EXPLORING COMPREHENSION

EXPLORING COMPREHENSION SKILLS: GRADE 4

INTRODUCTION

Teachers are under increasing pressure to ensure that their students are successful readers. The *Reading Next** report lists fifteen elements for improving literacy. *Exploring Comprehension Skills* incorporates several of these elements.

◆ **Direct, explicit comprehension instruction** . . . in the strategies and processes that proficient readers use to understand what they read

◆ **Effective instructional principles embedded in context** . . . providing instruction and practice in reading and writing skills specific to . . . content area

◆ **Motivation and self-directed learning** . . . providing students with the instruction and supports needed for independent learning tasks

◆ **Strategic tutoring**, which provides students with intense individualized reading, writing, and content instruction

◆ **Diverse texts** . . . at a variety of difficulty levels and on a variety of topics

Exploring Comprehension Skills provides instruction to help meet the needs of many students. The selections in this book cover a wide range of subjects in such areas as science, social studies, history, sports, and the arts. The high-interest fiction and nonfiction texts with low readability levels encourage readers to focus on skill development instead of reading obstructions.

ORGANIZATION

Exploring Comprehension Skills focuses on six of the most important reading comprehension skills: finding facts, recognizing sequence, understanding context, identifying main ideas, drawing conclusions, and making inferences.

◆ **Facts** Literal comprehension is a foundation skill for understanding a reading selection. Students using the Facts unit practice identifying pieces of information presented in each reading selection. The focus is on specific details that tell who, what, where, when, why, and how.

A facts lesson consists of a reading selection about a single topic broken into two parts. Each part is followed by five questions that require students to find restated facts from the selection.

◆ **Sequence** Sequence involves the time order of events and the temporal relationship of one event or step to other events or steps. Reading for sequence means identifying the order of events in a story or the steps in a process.

A sequence lesson consists of a reading selection about a single topic, followed by five questions. The first question asks students to put statements in order based on the information in each selection. The following questions ask about the stated or implied sequence in each selection.

◆ **Context** When students practice using context, they must use all the words in a reading selection to understand the unfamiliar words. As they develop this skill, students become aware of the relationships among words, phrases, and sentences. The skill provides them with a tool to help them understand words and concepts by learning how language is used to express meaning. Mastering this skill allows students to become independent readers.

A context lesson consists of four reading selections. In lessons 1 through 8, the selections are presented in a cloze format with one or two missing words. In lessons 9 through 16, the selection contains a word in boldface type. Students are asked to use the context of the selection to choose the correct definition for each boldfaced word.

◆ **Main Idea** When students read for the main idea, they must read to recognize the overall point made in the reading selection. Students must be able to differentiate the details from the main idea. They must understand the one idea that is supported by all the details in a selection, chapter, or paragraph. Identifying the main idea involves recognizing or making a generalization about a group of specifics.

A main idea lesson consists of three short reading selections for which students are asked to identify the main idea. Some selections have stated main ideas, while other selections have implied main ideas.

◆ **Conclusion** Drawing a conclusion is a complex reading skill because a conclusion is not usually stated in a reading passage. Students are asked to draw a conclusion based only on the information within a selection. They must put together the clues as if they were solving a puzzle.

A conclusion lesson contains three short reading selections for which students are asked to choose a conclusion that can logically be drawn from the information presented. Lessons 8 through 14 are more difficult because students are asked to identify a conclusion that cannot be drawn from the information presented.

◆ **Inference** Students make inferences by combining their own knowledge and experiences with what they read. They must consider all the facts in the reading selection. Then they must put those facts together with what they already know to make a reasonable inference about something that is not stated in the selection. Making an inference, another complex skill, requires students to go beyond the information in the text.

An inference lesson consists of three short reading selections. Factual and inferential statements follow each reading selection. Students must differentiate the facts in the selection from the inferences that logically can be made.

*Biancarosa, G., & Snow, C.E. (2004). *Reading next—A Vision for action and research in middle and high school literacy: A report to Carnegie Corporation of New York*. Washington, D.C.: Alliance for Excellent Education.

FEATURES

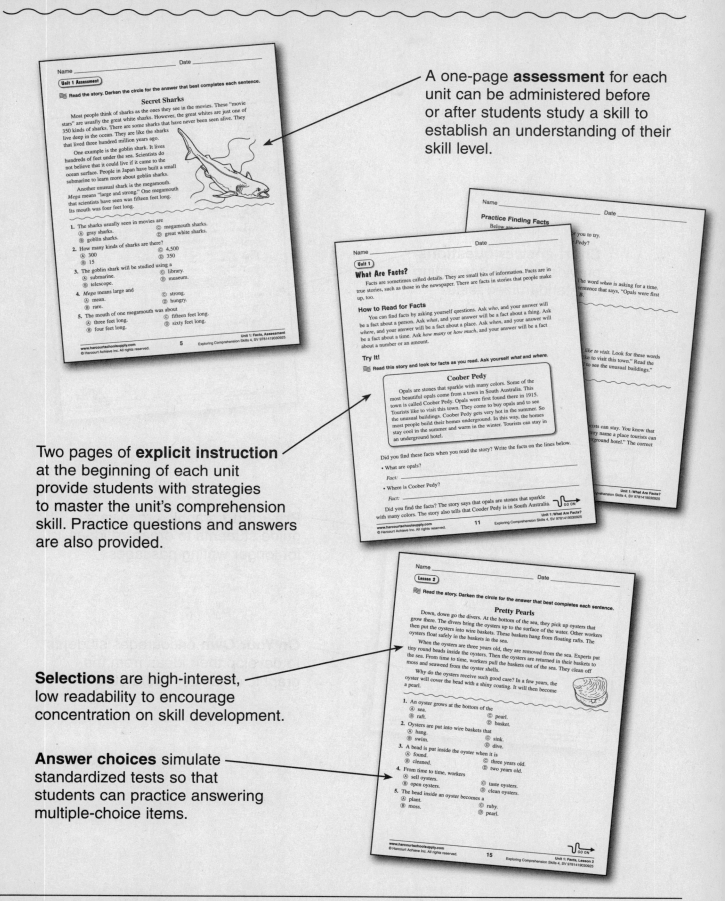

A one-page **assessment** for each unit can be administered before or after students study a skill to establish an understanding of their skill level.

Two pages of **explicit instruction** at the beginning of each unit provide students with strategies to master the unit's comprehension skill. Practice questions and answers are also provided.

Selections are high-interest, low readability to encourage concentration on skill development.

Answer choices simulate standardized tests so that students can practice answering multiple-choice items.

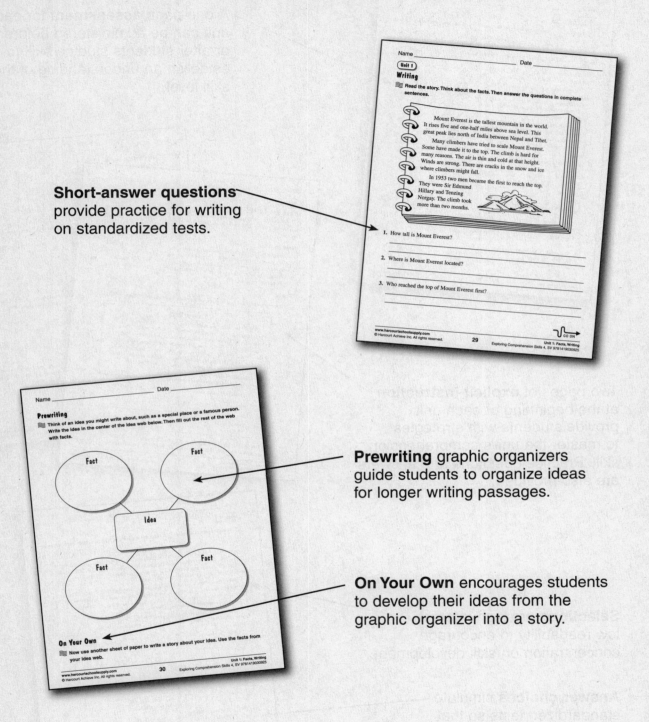

Short-answer questions provide practice for writing on standardized tests.

(Worksheet shown)

Name _____ Date _____

Unit 1
Writing

Read the story. Think about the facts. Then answer the questions in complete sentences.

Mount Everest is the tallest mountain in the world. It rises five and one-half miles above sea level. This great peak lies north of India between Nepal and Tibet.

Many climbers have tried to scale Mount Everest. Some have made it to the top. The climb is hard for many reasons. The air is thin and cold at that height. Winds are strong. There are cracks in the snow and ice where climbers might fall.

In 1953 two men became the first to reach the top. They were Sir Edmund Hillary and Tenzing Norgay. The climb took more than two months.

1. How tall is Mount Everest?
   _____

2. Where is Mount Everest located?
   _____

3. Who reached the top of Mount Everest first?
   _____

www.harcourtschoolsupply.com
© Harcourt Achieve Inc. All rights reserved.   29   Exploring Comprehension Skills 4, SV 9781419030925   Unit 1: Facts, Writing   GO ON

Prewriting graphic organizers guide students to organize ideas for longer writing passages.

(Worksheet shown)

Name _____ Date _____

Prewriting

Think of an idea you might write about, such as a special place or a famous person. Write the idea in the center of the idea web below. Then fill out the rest of the web with facts.

Fact — Fact — Idea — Fact — Fact

On Your Own
Now use another sheet of paper to write a story about your idea. Use the facts from your idea web.

www.harcourtschoolsupply.com
© Harcourt Achieve Inc. All rights reserved.   30   Exploring Comprehension Skills 4, SV 9781419030925   Unit 1: Facts, Writing

On Your Own encourages students to develop their ideas from the graphic organizer into a story.

Name _____ Date _____

≋ **Read the story. Darken the circle for the answer that best completes each sentence.**

Secret Sharks

Most people think of sharks as the ones they see in the movies. These "movie stars" are usually the great white sharks. However, the great whites are just one of 350 kinds of sharks. There are some sharks that have never been seen alive. They live deep in the ocean. They are like the sharks that lived three hundred million years ago.

One example is the goblin shark. It lives hundreds of feet under the sea. Scientists do not believe that it could live if it came to the ocean surface. People in Japan have built a small submarine to learn more about goblin sharks.

Another unusual shark is the megamouth. *Mega* means "large and strong." One megamouth that scientists have seen was fifteen feet long. Its mouth was four feet long.

1. The sharks usually seen in movies are
   Ⓐ gray sharks.
   Ⓑ goblin sharks.
   Ⓒ megamouth sharks.
   Ⓓ great white sharks.

2. How many kinds of sharks are there?
   Ⓐ 300
   Ⓑ 15
   Ⓒ 4,500
   Ⓓ 350

3. The goblin shark will be studied using a
   Ⓐ submarine.
   Ⓑ telescope.
   Ⓒ library.
   Ⓓ museum.

4. *Mega* means large and
   Ⓐ mean.
   Ⓑ rare.
   Ⓒ strong.
   Ⓓ hungry.

5. The mouth of one megamouth was about
   Ⓐ three feet long.
   Ⓑ four feet long.
   Ⓒ fifteen feet long.
   Ⓓ sixty feet long.

Name _____ Date _____

≋ **Read the story.**

Abe's "Tall" Tale

Abe Lincoln was the sixteenth President of the United States. Lincoln was a serious man, but he also had a funny side. He was famous for his jokes and funny stories.

When Abe began to grow as a boy, his stepmother teased him about his tall height. She would tell him to keep the top of his head clean. That way he wouldn't get her ceiling dirty. She told him that it was easy enough to wash the floor when it got dirty, but the ceiling was another matter. Abe took this teasing in good spirits.

Then one day Abe got an idea. He was watching some little boys playing in the mud. He noticed how dirty their feet were. Abe looked around. His stepmother wasn't home. So he went outside toward the boys in the mud puddle. He picked up one boy and carried him into the house. Then he went back and picked up another boy.

One by one, Abe turned the boys upside down. Then he walked their dirty feet across the clean, white ceiling. They made a trail of muddy footprints from one room to the other. The boys thought this was great fun, and so did Abe.

Then Abe waited for his stepmother to return. When she did, she saw the footprints right away. "Abe Lincoln, you've played a good joke on me!" she laughed. "I guess I deserve it."

〰〰〰〰〰〰〰〰〰〰〰〰〰〰〰〰〰〰〰〰〰〰〰〰〰〰〰〰〰〰〰〰〰

1. Put these events in the order that they happened. What happened first? Write the number **1** on the line by that sentence. Then write the number **2** by the sentence that tells what happened next. Write the number **3** by the sentence that tells what happened last.

    _____ Abe's stepmother teased him.

    _____ Abe brought the boys into the house.

    _____ Abe saw some little boys playing in the mud.

≋ **Darken the circle for the phrase that best answers each question.**

2. When did Abe carry the boys into the house?
    Ⓐ when he saw them playing outside in the mud
    Ⓑ after he walked their feet across the ceiling
    Ⓒ before he looked to see if his stepmother was around

Name _____ Date _____

≈ **Darken the circle for the word that best completes each sentence.**

People in Russia give eggs as gifts. They do not give just plain white eggs. The eggs are painted with pictures. Many of the pictures have _(1)_ meanings, such as "good luck" and "long life." In Russia, _(2)_ eggs become little works of art!

1. Ⓐ special   Ⓑ cold   Ⓒ small   Ⓓ purple

2. Ⓐ lizard   Ⓑ ordinary   Ⓒ red   Ⓓ broken

A man wondered whether bees know which flowers to go to. So he drew flowers on a large _(3)_ of paper. Half the flowers were blue. The other half were yellow. On each blue flower, he put a big cup of sugar water. But he put a _(4)_ cup on each yellow flower. The bees stopped going to the yellow flowers.

3. Ⓐ test   Ⓑ row   Ⓒ sheet   Ⓓ pencil

4. Ⓐ big   Ⓑ tiny   Ⓒ glass   Ⓓ slow

Animals have different ways to **escape** from danger. Some run very fast. Others climb trees. But some are safe because they are hard to see. They may be the same color as the ground. Or they may look like plants. They may have stripes or spots that look like the shadows of trees. Instead of running, these animals stand very still.

5. In this story, the word **escape** means
   Ⓐ hide.   Ⓑ leave.   Ⓒ chase.   Ⓓ jump.

Every year in Thailand, people have Elephant Day. They bring their elephants to one **location**. Everyone comes to see whose elephant is the best. The elephants run a race. They also carry big logs and stack them in a pile.

6. In this story, the word **location** means
   Ⓐ place.   Ⓑ parade.   Ⓒ street.   Ⓓ country.

Name _____ Date _____

≋ **Read the stories. Darken the circle for the phrase that best completes each sentence.**

Camp Fire is a group that helps young people. Both boys and girls can belong to it. Everyone in the group learns by doing things. Sometimes these young people camp outside and cook dinner over a fire. They also help people. At times they just have fun together. They learn how to share and make friends.

1. The story mainly tells
   - Ⓐ when young people have fun.
   - Ⓑ who cooks over a camp fire.
   - Ⓒ how young people learn from Camp Fire.
   - Ⓓ how only girls belong to the group.

Pet dogs do some things that wild dogs do. Wild dogs eat very quickly. They must eat quickly because the other animals can take their food away. Pet dogs don't usually have this problem, but they still eat quickly. Wild dogs have to make their own beds. So they walk around and around in the grass to make it flat. Pet dogs also turn around a few times before they lie down.

2. The story mainly tells
   - Ⓐ who walks around in circles.
   - Ⓑ how pet dogs and wild dogs are alike.
   - Ⓒ how wild dogs make their beds.
   - Ⓓ how pet dogs eat slowly.

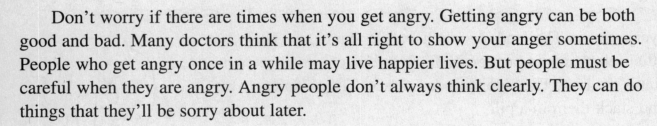

Don't worry if there are times when you get angry. Getting angry can be both good and bad. Many doctors think that it's all right to show your anger sometimes. People who get angry once in a while may live happier lives. But people must be careful when they are angry. Angry people don't always think clearly. They can do things that they'll be sorry about later.

3. The story mainly tells
   - Ⓐ why people can't think straight.
   - Ⓑ how people get angry about nothing.
   - Ⓒ how anger can be both good and bad.
   - Ⓓ how anger can make you sick.

Name _____ Date _____

≋ **Read the stories. Darken the circle for the phrase that best completes each sentence.**

Jay and Jean went to the store to buy toys for their baby. "Let's get a toy cat that has painted eyes," said Jay. "Button eyes can fall off, and the baby might eat them." They also wanted a wooden train set. Jean made sure that the train didn't have any sharp edges. They also bought a set of paints. The paints were marked *Safe for all ages*. Jay and Jean knew that their baby would like these toys.

1. From this story, you can tell that
    Ⓐ Jean was a painting teacher.
    Ⓑ Jean liked the train set the best.
    Ⓒ Jean and Jay bought only safe toys.
    Ⓓ Jean wanted a train with sharp edges.

People are always thinking of new things to sell in machines. Most machines sell candy and drinks. But now machines even sell flowers. Machines are placed where many people will see them. For instance, offices are a good place to put snack machines. Baseball parks are a good place for drink machines.

2. From this story, you can tell that
    Ⓐ drinks from a machine taste best.
    Ⓑ some machines sell things besides food.
    Ⓒ all drink machines are found in baseball parks.
    Ⓓ machines are placed where people won't see them.

Carla woke up when the rooster crowed. She lit a candle. Then she built a fire in the fireplace. The fire would help her make a good, warm breakfast. When Juan woke up, Carla sent him to gather more firewood. Juan also brought water from the well. After he ate, Juan walked the horses to the field to plow.

3. From this story, you can tell that
    Ⓐ Carla and Juan have many cows.
    Ⓑ Carla and Juan have six children.
    Ⓒ Carla and Juan probably live on a farm.
    Ⓓ Carla and Juan plow the fields together.

9

Name _____   Date _____

≋ **Read the stories. Darken the circle for the sentence that best answers each question.**

The village people chose a boy to guard the sheep. It was an important job.
If a wolf came near, the boy was supposed to call the people in the village. Then they
would come to help him. The boy watched the sheep for a little while. Then he decided
to have some fun. He cried out loudly, "Wolf! Wolf!" The people rushed out to fight
the wolf. When they arrived the boy was laughing at them.
There was no wolf.

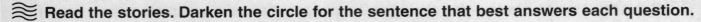

1. Which of these sentences is probably true?
   Ⓐ Everyone thought the joke was funny.
   Ⓑ Several of the sheep got lost.
   Ⓒ The people were angry at the boy.
   Ⓓ The boy was very kind.

In the 1950s, golf was a new sport in Japan. Many people liked the game. The
golfers practiced and practiced. They tried to hit the small, hard balls across the golf
course grass. But those who played golf were in great danger. In fact, people on the
golf course had to wear hard hats for their own safety.

2. Which of these sentences is probably true?
   Ⓐ Playing golf in the United States is not very safe.
   Ⓑ At first the golfers in Japan didn't play very well.
   Ⓒ People in Japan also played football.
   Ⓓ Golfers in Japan were often hit by lightning.

≋ **Read the stories. Darken the circle to show whether each statement is an inference
   or a fact.**

Jason and Josh were neighbors. They rode their bikes to school together every
day. Josh got a new bike for his birthday. Jason wished he had a new bike, too.
One day Josh left his bike in the yard. When he came back, it was gone.

3. FACT   INFERENCE
   ○   ○   A. Jason wanted a new bike.
   ○   ○   B. Josh and Jason rode to school together.
   ○   ○   C. Jason took Josh's bike.
   ○   ○   D. Josh and Jason were neighbors.

Unit 1

What Are Facts?

Facts are sometimes called details. They are small bits of information. Facts are in true stories, such as those in the newspaper. There are facts in stories that people make up, too.

How to Read for Facts

You can find facts by asking yourself questions. Ask *who*, and your answer will be a fact about a person. Ask *what*, and your answer will be a fact about a thing. Ask *where*, and your answer will be a fact about a place. Ask *when*, and your answer will be a fact about a time. Ask *how many* or *how much*, and your answer will be a fact about a number or an amount.

Try It!

 Read this story and look for facts as you read. Ask yourself *what* and *where*.

Coober Pedy

Opals are stones that sparkle with many colors. Some of the most beautiful opals come from a town in South Australia. This town is called Coober Pedy. Opals were first found there in 1915. Tourists like to visit this town. They come to buy opals and to see the unusual buildings. Coober Pedy gets very hot in the summer. So most people build their homes underground. In this way, the homes stay cool in the summer and warm in the winter. Tourists can stay in an underground hotel.

Did you find these facts when you read the story? Write the facts on the lines below.

• What are opals?

  Fact: _____

• Where is Coober Pedy?

  Fact: _____

Did you find the facts? The story says that opals are stones that sparkle with many colors. The story also tells that Cooder Pedy is in South Australia.

Practice Finding Facts

Below are some practice questions for you to try.

1. When were opals first found at Coober Pedy?
   - Ⓐ in 1991
   - Ⓑ in 1915
   - Ⓒ in summer
   - Ⓓ in winter

Look at the question and answers again. The word *when* is asking for a time. Reread the story and look for times. Find the sentence that says, "Opals were first found there in 1915." So the correct answer is **B**.

2. Tourists like to visit Coober Pedy
   - Ⓐ to swim.
   - Ⓑ to dig.
   - Ⓒ to buy opals.
   - Ⓓ to learn to cook.

Look at the question. It has the words *Tourists like to visit*. Look for these words in the story. You will find this sentence: "Tourists like to visit this town." Read the next sentence. It says, "They come to buy opals and to see the unusual buildings." The correct answer is **C**.

3. Where can tourists stay?
   - Ⓐ in a camp
   - Ⓑ in a house
   - Ⓒ in an apartment
   - Ⓓ in an underground hotel

Look at the question. *Where* asks for a place that tourists can stay. You know that tourists often stay at hotels. Look at the story. Does the story name a place tourists can stay? The last sentence says, "Tourists can stay in an underground hotel." The correct answer is **D**.

www.harcourtschoolsupply.com
© Harcourt Achieve Inc. All rights reserved.

12

Unit 1: What Are Facts?
Exploring Comprehension Skills 4, SV 9781419030925

Name _____   Date _____

≈ **Read the story. Darken the circle for the answer that best completes each sentence.**

Beard Beginnings

There's nothing really new about beards. Men have been growing beards for thousands of years. If a man does not shave his chin and the sides of his face, a beard will grow. Long ago all men had beards.

The first men to shave off their beards were the early Egyptians. But not all Egyptian men shaved. Some spent hours caring for their beards. They dyed them, braided them, and even wove gold threads into them. The kings and queens of Egypt sometimes wore false beards called postiches. A postiche was a sign of royalty. It was made of metal and attached to the chin with straps of gold.

Some men in ancient Greece wore beards. They thought a beard was a sign of wisdom. Socrates was a famous Greek who wore a beard. He was also thought to be a wise man.

1. If a man doesn't shave, he will grow a
   Ⓐ nose.   Ⓒ braid.
   Ⓑ beard.   Ⓓ chin.

2. Long ago all men had
   Ⓐ postiches.   Ⓒ gold.
   Ⓑ beards.   Ⓓ wisdom.

3. The kings of Egypt sometimes wore
   Ⓐ false beards.   Ⓒ diamond beards.
   Ⓑ wise beards.   Ⓓ cloth beards.

4. A postiche was a sign of
   Ⓐ weakness.   Ⓒ royalty.
   Ⓑ loyalty.   Ⓓ marriage.

5. A famous Greek who wore a beard was
   Ⓐ Postiche.   Ⓒ Egyptian.
   Ⓑ Burnside.   Ⓓ Socrates.

 GO ON

For hundreds of years, beards were not popular. They became fashionable again in the 1500s. One style of beard was called the goatee. This small, pointed beard hangs from the lower lip and chin. It looks like the beard of a goat. In the 1600s, another style of beard became popular. It was called the Vandyke. This beard was named after a famous painter of the time, Anthony Vandyke.

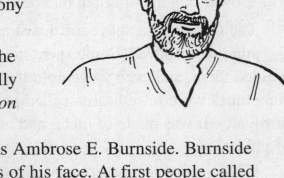

Men wore their whiskers in still other ways in the 1800s. Some men wore muttonchops. These are really side whiskers that are shaped like lamb chops. *Mutton* is another word for *lamb*. Another style was named after a general from the United States. His name was Ambrose E. Burnside. Burnside shaved his chin but grew short whiskers on the sides of his face. At first people called these burnsides. Later the name got mixed up and became *sideburns*.

6. The goatee became the fashion in the
   Ⓐ 1400s.
   Ⓒ 1700s.
   Ⓑ 1500s.
   Ⓓ 1800s.

7. The Vandyke beard was named after a
   Ⓐ general.
   Ⓒ painter.
   Ⓑ king.
   Ⓓ lamb.

8. Muttonchops are really
   Ⓐ postiches.
   Ⓒ chin whiskers.
   Ⓑ lambs.
   Ⓓ side whiskers.

9. Sideburns were named for an American
   Ⓐ officer.
   Ⓒ lamb chop.
   Ⓑ artist.
   Ⓓ mutton.

10. Sideburns were popular in the
    Ⓐ 1500s.
    Ⓒ 1700s.
    Ⓑ 1600s.
    Ⓓ 1800s.

≈ **Read the story. Darken the circle for the answer that best completes each sentence.**

Pretty Pearls

Down, down go the divers. At the bottom of the sea, they pick up oysters that grow there. The divers bring the oysters up to the surface of the water. Other workers then put the oysters into wire baskets. These baskets hang from floating rafts. The oysters float safely in the baskets in the sea.

When the oysters are three years old, they are removed from the sea. Experts put tiny round beads inside the oysters. Then the oysters are returned in their baskets to the sea. From time to time, workers pull the baskets out of the sea. They clean off moss and seaweed from the oyster shells.

Why do the oysters receive such good care? In a few years, the oyster will cover the bead with a shiny coating. It will then become a pearl.

1. An oyster grows at the bottom of the
   Ⓐ sea.   Ⓒ pearl.
   Ⓑ raft.   Ⓓ basket.

2. Oysters are put into wire baskets that
   Ⓐ hang.   Ⓒ sink.
   Ⓑ swim.   Ⓓ dive.

3. A bead is put inside the oyster when it is
   Ⓐ found.   Ⓒ three years old.
   Ⓑ cleaned.   Ⓓ two years old.

4. From time to time, workers
   Ⓐ sell oysters.   Ⓒ taste oysters.
   Ⓑ open oysters.   Ⓓ clean oysters.

5. The bead inside an oyster becomes a
   Ⓐ plant.   Ⓒ ruby.
   Ⓑ moss.   Ⓓ pearl.

Exploring Comprehension Skills 4, SV 9781419030925

The story of pearls goes back to 2206 B.C. That is more than four thousand years ago. At that time, people in China gave pearls as gifts or rewards. Pearls were used to decorate clay pots in Persia. In many countries, people thought of pearls as jewels of love. Husbands gave them to their wives. Kings and queens gave them to one another.

Over the years, people have used pearls in many ways. They have decorated crowns and swords with them. They have sewn pearls into fine clothing. Most often people have used pearls in pins, necklaces, rings, and bracelets.

The pearl is the birthstone for people who are born in June. The pearl is said to stand for health, wealth, and a long life. Perhaps that is why many people say that pearls become more beautiful with age.

6. Early Chinese people gave pearls as
   Ⓐ presents.
   Ⓑ baskets.
   Ⓒ kings.
   Ⓓ birthstones.

7. Long ago in Persia, pearls were used on
   Ⓐ walls.
   Ⓑ gifts.
   Ⓒ oysters.
   Ⓓ pottery.

8. People often use pearls in
   Ⓐ pottery.
   Ⓑ flowers.
   Ⓒ jewelry.
   Ⓓ baskets.

9. Pearls are birthstones for the month of
   Ⓐ April.
   Ⓑ June.
   Ⓒ July.
   Ⓓ December.

10. As pearls age, many people think they are
    Ⓐ more costly.
    Ⓑ less helpful.
    Ⓒ less valuable.
    Ⓓ more lovely.

Name _____   Date _____

≋ **Read the story. Darken the circle for the answer that best completes each sentence.**

Shivering Is Not Just Quivering

Have you ever shivered on a cold day? You may not have noticed, but as you shivered, your body warmed up. Shivering is one way your body stays warm. It happens when signals are sent from the nervous system to the muscles. This is how it works.

The nervous system has two parts. One part is the nerves. They look like long, thin threads. Their job is to carry messages to all parts of the body. The spinal cord and the brain make up the other part of the nervous system. The spinal cord is a large bundle of nerves inside the backbone. Signals from the brain travel down the spinal cord. They go to the rest of the body through the nerves. Muscles receive these signals.

1. Shivering helps your body
   - Ⓐ keep calm.
   - Ⓑ stay warm.
   - Ⓒ cool down.
   - Ⓓ stand up straight.

2. Signals go from the nervous system to
   - Ⓐ the muscles.
   - Ⓑ a certain cell.
   - Ⓒ the legs.
   - Ⓓ the nerves.

3. The nervous system has
   - Ⓐ one part.
   - Ⓑ three parts.
   - Ⓒ two parts.
   - Ⓓ many parts.

4. Nerves look like
   - Ⓐ muscles.
   - Ⓑ threads.
   - Ⓒ blood cells.
   - Ⓓ small trees.

5. The spinal cord is a large bundle of
   - Ⓐ muscles.
   - Ⓑ brain cells.
   - Ⓒ nerves.
   - Ⓓ signals.

Imagine waiting for a bus on a street corner. It's a cold day, the bus is late, and you feel chilled. Here's what happens.

A control center in your brain senses that you're cold. It sends a message down the spinal cord to all the nerves. The message races through nerves that connect to other nerves. Then it goes from the nerves to the muscles. The message says, "Warning! Prepare for action!"

When a muscle moves, it makes heat. That is why you get warm when you run or play soccer. When your muscles get the signal that you are cold, they get busy. First they become tight, and then they loosen. They tighten then loosen over and over again. This makes you shiver. You also get warmer.

6. Your brain's signal travels first to the
   Ⓐ bus.
   Ⓑ spinal cord.
   Ⓒ heart.
   Ⓓ muscles.

7. Nerves tell the muscles to
   Ⓐ stop.
   Ⓑ relax.
   Ⓒ get ready.
   Ⓓ cool down.

8. When a muscle moves, it becomes
   Ⓐ warm.
   Ⓑ cool.
   Ⓒ stiff.
   Ⓓ heavy.

9. When you become cold, your muscles
   Ⓐ relax.
   Ⓑ stretch.
   Ⓒ stop moving.
   Ⓓ tighten and loosen.

10. When you shiver, you get
    Ⓐ weaker.
    Ⓑ colder.
    Ⓒ stronger.
    Ⓓ warmer.

Lesson 4

≈ **Read the story. Darken the circle for the answer that best completes each sentence.**

Bring More Water, Molly Pitcher

Molly Ludwig was a young girl when she met John Hays. She married him before she turned 15. They lived a quiet life in Pennsylvania. John worked as a barber, and Molly took care of their son.

Then their peaceful life changed. Many people felt that it was time for America to win its freedom from British rule. Along with his friends and neighbors, John joined the army.

Molly followed John into war. Like many young wives of the day, she washed and cooked for him while he fought in the war. She and John put up with the hardships of army life for three years.

1. Molly married John before she was
   Ⓐ 19.
   Ⓑ 14.
   Ⓒ 15.
   Ⓓ 20.

2. John worked as a
   Ⓐ lawyer.
   Ⓑ doctor.
   Ⓒ saddle maker.
   Ⓓ barber.

3. Many people felt America should
   Ⓐ make laws.
   Ⓑ make money.
   Ⓒ win its freedom.
   Ⓓ collect taxes.

4. John joined the
   Ⓐ British.
   Ⓑ army.
   Ⓒ local club.
   Ⓓ barber school.

5. While John fought the war, Molly
   Ⓐ rode horses.
   Ⓑ visited friends.
   Ⓒ laughed and played.
   Ⓓ washed and cooked.

⤴ **GO ON**

Molly was given a nickname by George Washington's troops. She hauled water to the men as they fought in battles. She carried the water in pitchers. One hot day as the men drank the cool water, they gave Molly her new name. They called her Molly Pitcher.

As she worked, Molly watched John fight. He was forcing cannonballs into a cannon with a long pole. All at once she saw him fall to the ground. She could tell he was hurt as he was moved off the field. Molly rushed to take his place at the cannon. She grabbed the pole and started to work. The battle went on as Molly fought in John's place. After the battle, Molly joined the army. She served as a soldier for almost eight years.

6. Molly earned her nickname by hauling
    Ⓐ water.   Ⓒ cannons.
    Ⓑ logs.   Ⓓ meat.

7. Molly helped the soldiers during
    Ⓐ meals.   Ⓒ illness.
    Ⓑ marches.   Ⓓ battles.

8. John put cannonballs in the cannon with
    Ⓐ a door.   Ⓒ a pitcher.
    Ⓑ water.   Ⓓ a long pole.

9. When John fell, Molly took his
    Ⓐ pitcher.   Ⓒ place.
    Ⓑ horse.   Ⓓ hat.

10. After the battle, Molly became a
    Ⓐ teacher.   Ⓒ nurse.
    Ⓑ soldier.   Ⓓ pilot.

Lesson 5

≋ **Read the story. Darken the circle for the answer that best completes each sentence.**

Made for the Job

If you looked at a bald eagle, it would stare back at you. But the eagle would see you more clearly than you see it. Birds can see better than other animals, and eagles can see better than other birds. An eagle can see three to eight times better than a human can. This helps it with its main job, hunting. While an eagle glides high in the air, it can spot a fish in a stream far below.

An eagle must fly great distances in search of food. Its wings also help it hunt. When an eagle's wings are spread out, they stretch out six or seven feet. These large wings can carry an eagle over a hundred miles in a day.

1. If you looked at a bald eagle, it would
   - Ⓐ squawk.
   - Ⓑ blink.
   - Ⓒ fly away.
   - Ⓓ stare back.

2. An eagle's sharp eyes help it
   - Ⓐ sleep.
   - Ⓑ hunt.
   - Ⓒ find a mate.
   - Ⓓ fly.

3. While it is flying, an eagle looks for
   - Ⓐ food.
   - Ⓑ humans.
   - Ⓒ feathers.
   - Ⓓ other eagles.

4. An eagle's wings can measure
   - Ⓐ three feet.
   - Ⓑ five feet.
   - Ⓒ fifteen feet.
   - Ⓓ seven feet.

5. In a day, an eagle can fly more than
   - Ⓐ 600 miles.
   - Ⓑ 700 miles.
   - Ⓒ 100 miles.
   - Ⓓ 1,000 miles.

GO ON

When a hungry eagle sees a fish, it swoops down at top speed
toward the stream. Then it snatches the fish with its sharp claws.
These claws are called talons. The talons are at least one inch long.
They grasp the fish tightly as the eagle soars upward. The toes and the
bottoms of the eagle's feet are covered with hundreds of tiny bumps.
These bumps help it hold the slippery fish.

The eagle might carry the fish to shore. There the eagle's pointed beak helps it eat
the fish. An eagle uses its beak to catch prey and to tear meat.

6. When a hungry eagle sees a fish, it
   - Ⓐ calls out.
   - Ⓑ dives.
   - Ⓒ flies higher.
   - Ⓓ flies away.

7. An eagle picks up its food with its
   - Ⓐ feet.
   - Ⓑ wings.
   - Ⓒ eyes.
   - Ⓓ feathers.

8. An eagle's talons
   - Ⓐ help it see.
   - Ⓑ are not sharp.
   - Ⓒ help it fly.
   - Ⓓ catch its food.

9. The tiny bumps on an eagle's feet help it
   - Ⓐ fly.
   - Ⓑ see.
   - Ⓒ hold its food.
   - Ⓓ soar upward.

10. An eagle's pointed beak helps it to
    - Ⓐ fly.
    - Ⓑ eat.
    - Ⓒ crack seeds.
    - Ⓓ grab branches.

Lesson 6

≈ **Read the story. Darken the circle for the answer that best completes each sentence.**

Louis Braille

Louis Braille was born in a small French town. When he was three, he lost his sight. At ten he went to a school for children who were blind. The books at his school were written with raised letters. He moved his fingers over the letters to read the books. But letters like *A* and *H* felt the same. He had a hard time understanding what he read.

Then Louis learned of a different way to read. It was used by soldiers who had to read messages in the dark. To write the messages, people punched dots in paper. Since the dots were raised, people could feel them.

Braille Alphabet

a	b	c	d	e	f	g	h	i	j
1	2	3	4	5	6	7	8	9	0

| k | l | m | n | o | p | q | r | s | t |

| u | v | w | x | y | z | | Capital Sign | Numeral Sign |

1. Louis Braille was born in
   - Ⓐ Spain.
   - Ⓒ England.
   - Ⓑ France.
   - Ⓓ the United States.

2. Louis lost his sight when he was
   - Ⓐ two.
   - Ⓒ ten.
   - Ⓑ three.
   - Ⓓ fifteen.

3. To read books Louis used
   - Ⓐ his fingers.
   - Ⓒ a machine.
   - Ⓑ his eyes.
   - Ⓓ his mother's help.

4. Louis had a hard time understanding
   - Ⓐ his friends.
   - Ⓒ what he heard.
   - Ⓑ his teachers.
   - Ⓓ what he read.

5. The system with raised dots was used by
   - Ⓐ miners.
   - Ⓒ doctors.
   - Ⓑ soldiers.
   - Ⓓ forest rangers.

GO ON

Exploring Comprehension Skills 4, SV 9781419030925

Louis liked the idea of reading with raised dots. But he thought it could be made simpler. So when Louis was fifteen, he made up a new way of writing. He used raised dots, but he made up his own alphabet.

All of Louis's friends at school liked his idea. But many teachers did not want to use it. They thought the old way worked just fine. Then in 1844 this new way of reading and writing was shown to the public. When more people saw how it worked, they liked it. Today people all over the world read books written in Braille.

6. Louis decided to use the idea of reading
   - (A) old books.
   - (B) aloud.
   - (C) raised dots.
   - (D) picture books.

7. Louis's new system used
   - (A) small letters.
   - (B) a machine.
   - (C) no raised dots.
   - (D) a new alphabet.

8. Louis's friends thought his system
   - (A) was strange.
   - (B) was too hard.
   - (C) worked well.
   - (D) did not work.

9. At first the new system was not used by
   - (A) parents.
   - (B) students.
   - (C) the government.
   - (D) people who taught school.

10. Today Braille's system
    - (A) is not used.
    - (B) is well liked.
    - (C) does not work.
    - (D) is used only in France.

Exploring Comprehension Skills 4, SV 9781419030925

Lesson 7

≋ **Read the story. Darken the circle for the answer that best completes each sentence.**

Her Honor

The United States Supreme Court is the highest court of the land. For many years, only men were Supreme Court justices. That was true until 1981. That year Sandra Day O'Connor became a Supreme Court justice. She was the first woman to do so.

Sandra's first teacher was her mother. Later Sandra went to school. Sandra finished high school when she was just sixteen. Then she followed her dream to study law. She was in law school for five years. When she finished law school, she couldn't find a job. Very few companies wanted women who knew law!

1. The highest court of the land is the
   - Ⓐ World Court.
   - Ⓑ State Court.
   - Ⓒ Supreme Court.
   - Ⓓ United States Court.

2. Only men served on the Supreme Court
   - Ⓐ after 1990.
   - Ⓑ after 1811.
   - Ⓒ until 1981.
   - Ⓓ until 200 years ago.

3. Sandra's first teacher was her
   - Ⓐ mother.
   - Ⓑ father.
   - Ⓒ sister.
   - Ⓓ grandmother.

4. Sandra's dream was to
   - Ⓐ go to school.
   - Ⓑ study law.
   - Ⓒ stay at home.
   - Ⓓ work on a ranch.

5. When Sandra finished law school, she
   - Ⓐ found a job.
   - Ⓑ got sick.
   - Ⓒ couldn't find a job.
   - Ⓓ went back to school.

〰️ **GO ON** →

Sandra married a man she met in law school. They both got jobs as lawyers. For a while, Sandra had her own law office. Then she and her husband had a son. Sandra decided to stay home. Sandra and her husband had two more sons.

After nine years, Sandra became a judge in Arizona. She was a judge there for seven years. Then one of the justices from the Supreme Court left. So the Supreme Court needed another justice. The President of the United States heard about Sandra. He asked her to become a justice on the Supreme Court. Sandra eagerly said, "Yes!"

6. Sandra and her husband were both
   Ⓐ doctors.
   Ⓑ lawyers.
   Ⓒ teachers.
   Ⓓ bankers.

7. Sandra had
   Ⓐ three sons.
   Ⓑ two daughters.
   Ⓒ a son and a daughter.
   Ⓓ four children.

8. Sandra stayed home with her children for
   Ⓐ nine years.
   Ⓑ seven years.
   Ⓒ twenty years.
   Ⓓ five years.

9. One of the justices left the
   Ⓐ High Court.
   Ⓑ World Court.
   Ⓒ Arizona Court.
   Ⓓ Supreme Court.

10. The president asked Sandra to be a
    Ⓐ student.
    Ⓑ lawyer.
    Ⓒ justice in an Arizona court.
    Ⓓ justice on the Supreme Court.

Name _____   Date _____

≋ **Read the story. Darken the circle for the answer that best completes each sentence.**

Good Night, Don't Bite!

There's nothing quite like falling sound asleep after a full day of work. Like people, animals need to rest after working hard. Some animals sleep floating in water. Others dig holes under the ground. Some even sleep high in trees or under leaves. But they all find a way to rest.

Animals sleeping in the sea can be a strange sight. Fish sleep with their eyes open. They do not have eyelids, so they seem to stare into the depths while they nap. Sea otters sometimes sleep in beds of seaweed. This keeps them from floating away. Parrotfish blow a clear gel from their mouths when they are ready to snooze. The gel forms a bubble around them. The bubble protects them from harm while they sleep.

1. Like people, animals need to
   Ⓐ cry.
   Ⓑ talk.
   Ⓒ rest.
   Ⓓ tell time.

2. Fish do not have
   Ⓐ scales.
   Ⓑ bubbles.
   Ⓒ tails.
   Ⓓ eyelids.

3. Sea otters sometimes sleep in
   Ⓐ holes.
   Ⓑ seaweed.
   Ⓒ boats.
   Ⓓ caves.

4. Parrotfish make a clear gel with their
   Ⓐ mouths.
   Ⓑ scales.
   Ⓒ skin.
   Ⓓ fins.

5. Parrotfish sleep in a bubble that
   Ⓐ shrinks.
   Ⓑ glows.
   Ⓒ grows large.
   Ⓓ protects them.

↪ **GO ON**

Other animals sleep under the ground. Chipmunks sleep curled up in a ball. Their beds are made of leaves and grass. They wake up now and then to snack on food stored nearby. Some desert frogs dig underground holes during the hot, dry season. A frog may stay in its hole for months.

High above the ground, monkeys make leafy nests in trees each evening before they retire. The tree's high branches help to keep the monkeys safe during the night. Even the insects buzzing around their heads rest. Some sleep under a leaf that will be their next meal. A bee might crawl down into a blossom to rest. When it crawls out the next morning, it is rested and ready to buzz off to work.

6. Chipmunks sleep in beds made of
   Ⓐ nets.
   Ⓑ mud.
   Ⓒ leaves and grass.
   Ⓓ sticks and twigs.

7. Desert frogs stay underground during
   Ⓐ morning.
   Ⓑ winter.
   Ⓒ the night.
   Ⓓ the hot, dry season.

8. Monkeys make beds using material from
   Ⓐ insects.
   Ⓑ water.
   Ⓒ the ground.
   Ⓓ trees.

9. Some insects rest
   Ⓐ while eating.
   Ⓑ under leaves.
   Ⓒ while buzzing.
   Ⓓ curled up in a ball.

10. A bee might sleep in
    Ⓐ a flower.
    Ⓑ mud.
    Ⓒ a bubble.
    Ⓓ clear gel.

Name _____ Date _____

Writing

 Read the story. Think about the facts. Then answer the questions in complete sentences.

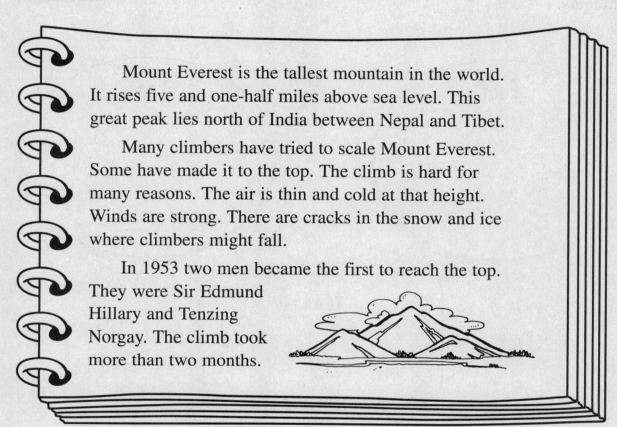

Mount Everest is the tallest mountain in the world. It rises five and one-half miles above sea level. This great peak lies north of India between Nepal and Tibet.

Many climbers have tried to scale Mount Everest. Some have made it to the top. The climb is hard for many reasons. The air is thin and cold at that height. Winds are strong. There are cracks in the snow and ice where climbers might fall.

In 1953 two men became the first to reach the top. They were Sir Edmund Hillary and Tenzing Norgay. The climb took more than two months.

1. How tall is Mount Everest?

_____

_____

2. Where is Mount Everest located?

_____

_____

3. Who reached the top of Mount Everest first?

_____

_____

GO ON

Prewriting

≈ Think of an idea you might write about, such as a special place or a famous person. Write the idea in the center of the idea web below. Then fill out the rest of the web with facts.

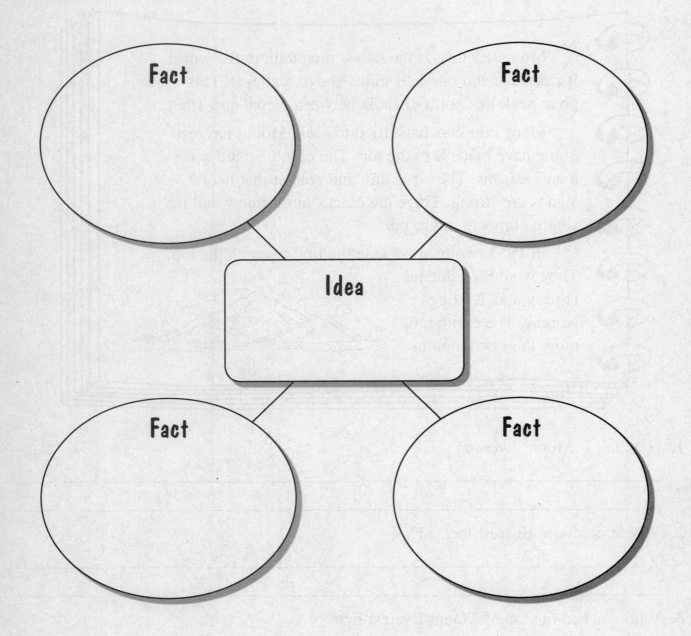

On Your Own

≈ Now use another sheet of paper to write a story about your idea. Use the facts from your idea web.

Unit 2

What Is Sequence?

Sequence means time order. Events in a story happen in a sequence. Something happens first. Then other things happen.

How can you find the sequence in a story? Look for time words such as *first*, *next*, and *last*. Here is a list of time words:

later	during	days of the week
today	while	months of the year

Try It!

 Follow the sequence in this story. Circle all the time words.

> Long ago a woodcutter and his wife lived in the forest. One day he found a lovely white crane caught in a trap. He freed the crane and went back to work. That night a young girl knocked on the couple's door. They took her inside. The next day, she gave them a beautiful woven cloth and told them to sell it for a high price. Each day she gave them a new cloth. On the seventh night, the woodcutter woke up. He saw a crane at the loom weaving cloth from its feathers. The crane said, "I came here to repay you for saving me. But now I must go." It said good-bye and then flew away.

Try putting these events in the order they happened. What happened first? Write the number **1** on the line by that sentence. Then write the number **2** by the sentence that tells what happened next. Write the number **3** by the sentence that tells what happened last.

_____ A young girl knocked on the couple's door.

_____ The woodcutter freed the crane from a trap.

_____ The girl gave the couple beautiful cloth.

Reread the story to review the sequence. Check your answers. The correct sequence is 2, 1, 3.

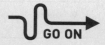

www.harcourtschoolsupply.com
© Harcourt Achieve Inc. All rights reserved.

31

Unit 2: What Is Sequence?
Exploring Comprehension Skills 4, SV 9781419030925

Practice with Sequence

Here are some practice questions. Darken the circle by the correct answer.

1. When did the woodcutter see the crane at the loom?
   Ⓐ that evening
   Ⓑ at noon on the second day
   Ⓒ on the seventh night

   Look at the question. Find the words *at the loom* in the story. They are in the sentence "He saw a crane at the loom weaving cloth from its feathers." The sentence before this one will tell you when he saw the crane. It says, "On the seventh night, the woodcutter woke up." So **C** is the correct answer. The man saw the crane at the loom on the seventh night.

2. What happened just before the crane flew away?
   Ⓐ The crane gave a cry of pain.
   Ⓑ The crane said good-bye.
   Ⓒ The crane wove cloth from its feathers.

   Look at the question carefully. Notice the time word *before*. Also notice the word *just*. The question asks what happened *just before* the crane flew away. The sentence "It said good-bye and then flew away" tells you. The last thing the crane did before flying away was to say good-bye. So **B** is the correct answer.

3. When did the crane weave the cloth?
   Ⓐ during the night
   Ⓑ in the morning
   Ⓒ in the afternoon

   Can you find the answer? The correct answer is **A**. Tell why. Write your ideas on the lines below.

   _____

   _____

   _____

   _____

   _____

Name _____ Date _____

Name _____ Date _____

Lesson 1

≋ **Read the story.**

Making Chocolate Candy

A chocolate candy bar is easy to eat, but it is hard to make. Chocolate fruits grow on trees in countries where the climate is hot. The fruits grow on the trunks of the trees. When these fruits are as big as bowling balls, workers cut them down. Workers split the shells and remove the chocolate beans. They lay the beans outside in the sun and cover them with banana leaves. Later workers uncover the beans to dry them. When the beans are very dry, workers put them in bags. These bags of beans are sent to other countries to be made into candy.

First the candy maker uses machines to clean the dry beans. Next the beans are heated and ground. Huge machines press a chocolate butter from these ground beans.

Now the candy making starts. Machines mix the ground beans with more chocolate butter. To make milk chocolate, the candy maker adds milk and sugar. Then this mixture is put into another machine. The mixture is squeezed until it becomes a soft paste. Next this candy paste is put into a big, stone pan. Large, round stones rub the paste. This rubbing helps stir the chocolate. It also removes any lumps.

After hours of rubbing, the candy is almost ready. Fruits or nuts may be added now. The candy is made into bars. When the bars have cooled, they are wrapped. They are then packed and sent to the stores.

GO ON

1. Put these events in the order that they happened. What happened first? Write the number **1** on the line by that sentence. Then write the number **2** by the sentence that tells what happened next. Write the number **3** by the sentence that tells what happened last.

   _____ Workers dry the beans.

   _____ Workers take the beans out of their shells.

   _____ Workers put the beans in bags.

≋ **Darken the circle for the phrase that best answers each question.**

2. Which machine are the chocolate beans put into first?
   Ⓐ a mixing machine
   Ⓑ a butter-pressing machine
   Ⓒ a cleaning machine

3. When does the candy making start?
   Ⓐ when the ground beans are mixed with the chocolate butter
   Ⓑ when the candy paste is rubbed with stones
   Ⓒ when the candy is shaped into bars

4. When are fruits or nuts added to the chocolate bars?
   Ⓐ when the bars are wrapped for shipping
   Ⓑ before the candy is shaped into bars
   Ⓒ while the candy is being cleaned

5. When is the candy sent to the stores?
   Ⓐ while the candy is cooling
   Ⓑ before the candy has been wrapped
   Ⓒ after the candy has been packed

≋ **Read the story.**

Trapped!

It was December 1984. A large herd of hungry white whales was chasing codfish. The whales chased the codfish from the sea into the Senyavin Strait. This narrow body of water separates an island from the coast of Russia.

An angry east wind blew. The water began to freeze. Soon the strait was jammed with ice that was up to twelve feet thick. Only small pools of open water remained. The whales were trapped in the strait!

A hunter spotted the whales and saw that they were in trouble. White whales can break through thin ice, but this ice was too thick. The hunter knew that whales must rise to the water's surface in order to breathe. There just wasn't enough room for thousands of these ten-foot whales to breathe. Soon there were helicopters on the scene. They dropped frozen fish to feed the whales. But the whales still could not breathe. They were beginning to die. The helpers sent for a special ship. Spotter planes helped the ship find the right place in which to ram through the ice. At first the whales just rested in the big pools that the ship made. Then as the whales became stronger, they began to play.

This was not what the captain of the ship wanted. He knew that the water would freeze again. Somehow he had to get the whales to follow the ship out to sea. Finally someone remembered that porpoises like music. Whales are related to porpoises. Maybe they would like music, too. So the crew of the ship played all kinds of music on deck. The whales liked classical music best.

Slowly they began to follow the ship. It took a long time to get the whales out of the strait. The ship would break the ice and then wait for the whales. After a while, the whales got used to the ship. They swam around the ship on all sides. By February the white whales were safely in the sea again.

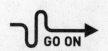
GO ON

1. Put these events in the order that they happened. What happened first? Write the number **1** on the line by that sentence. Then write the number **2** by the sentence that tells what happened next. Write the number **3** by the sentence that tells what happened last.

_____ The whales were trapped.

_____ The east wind blew.

_____ The whales entered the strait.

≋ **Darken the circle for the phrase that best answers each question.**

2. When were the whales trapped?
   Ⓐ after they followed the codfish
   Ⓑ before December
   Ⓒ after the icebreaker arrived

3. When did the ship arrive?
   Ⓐ after helicopters flew over
   Ⓑ while the whales played
   Ⓒ after the thick ice had melted

4. What did the special ship do first?
   Ⓐ led the whales to safety
   Ⓑ played classical music
   Ⓒ rammed the ice

5. When were the whales in the strait?
   Ⓐ from December to February
   Ⓑ from Saturday through Friday
   Ⓒ from February to December

Exploring Comprehension Skills 4, SV 9781419030925

Lesson 3

≋ **Read the story.**

Sequoyah

Sequoyah's people, the Cherokees, did not know how to write. They did not have an alphabet. They could not read books. Sequoyah wanted to draw some letters for the Cherokees.

First he drew pictures on tree bark. He needed a new picture for each word. He was so busy that he had no time to hunt. His garden of corn and beans died. One day Sequoyah's wife burned all his bark pictures. Sequoyah became very angry. He took his daughter, Ah-Yoka, and went away.

Later the two found a book written in English. Sequoyah saw that there were only 26 different marks. He realized that he didn't need a picture for each word. He just needed a mark for each sound. So he started all over again.

Finally the work was done. He taught the letters to Ah-Yoka. Then he talked to the Cherokee leaders about his work. They did not believe him. They wanted to test the letters.

The leaders told Sequoyah, "You go away for a little while. We will talk with your daughter. Then she will write a letter to you. When you return, you must read the letter to us. The words must be the words we told your daughter." Sequoyah was worried. Ah-Yoka was only ten years old. He went away and waited.

Later the leaders called him back. He picked up the letter and read the words out loud. The words were the same words that the leaders had used. Sequoyah's idea had worked!

GO ON

1. Put these events in the order that they happened. What happened first? Write the number **1** on the line by that sentence. Then write the number **2** by the sentence that tells what happened next. Write the number **3** by the sentence that tells what happened last.

_____ Ah-Yoka wrote down the words of the leaders.

_____ Sequoyah read Ah-Yoka's letter.

_____ The leaders talked with Ah-Yoka.

≈ **Darken the circle for the phrase that best answers each question.**

2. When did Ah-Yoka and Sequoyah find a book written in English?
   Ⓐ after Sequoyah moved away from his wife
   Ⓑ before he started drawing pictures for words
   Ⓒ after the Cherokee leaders sent him away

3. When did Ah-Yoka write a letter to Sequoyah?
   Ⓐ before he saw the marks in English
   Ⓑ before his wife got angry at him
   Ⓒ after he talked with the Cherokee leaders

4. When did the leaders think that Sequoyah's idea could work?
   Ⓐ before his wife burned the bark pictures
   Ⓑ after he read Ah-Yoka's letter
   Ⓒ before the leaders talked with Ah-Yoka

5. When did Sequoyah realize that he needed only a mark for each sound?
   Ⓐ before he drew pictures on tree bark
   Ⓑ after he taught the letters to Ah-Yoka
   Ⓒ after he saw 26 marks in English

Exploring Comprehension Skills 4, SV 9781419030925

Lesson 4

≋ **Read the story.**

The Space Shuttle

Shuttle means "to go back and forth." The space shuttle was designed to go back and forth between Earth and space. The first shuttle flight was on April 12, 1981.

The space shuttle has four main parts. It has an orbiter, a fuel tank, and two rocket boosters. The orbiter is like an airplane. It carries the crew. It has its own engines. The orbiter is the part of the shuttle that goes all the way around Earth.

The orbiter is attached to a huge tank. This tank holds fuel for its engines. On each side of the tank is a rocket booster. These rockets fire up on liftoff. In two minutes, they run out of fuel. They fall from the orbiter. Parachutes slow their fall to the sea. Then boats tow the rockets to shore. The rockets can be used again as many as twenty times.

After eight minutes, the big tank runs out of fuel. It falls and breaks into pieces over the sea. Now only the orbiter is left. It enters its orbit in space. It may have as many as seven crew members on board. Often the crew members launch satellites. Sometimes they work on experiments.

When it is time to come back to Earth, the orbiter's engines are fired. This slows the spacecraft down. It drops from orbit. Tiles protect the shuttle from the heat caused by entering Earth's atmosphere. The spacecraft now acts like a plane. The shuttle glides to a landing on a runway.

1. Put these events in the order that they happened. What happened first? Write the number **1** on the line by that sentence. Then write the number **2** by the sentence that tells what happened next. Write the number **3** by the sentence that tells what happened last.

_____ The shuttle drops from orbit.

_____ The orbiter's engines are fired.

_____ The shuttle glides to a landing.

≋ **Darken the circle for the phrase that best answers each question.**

2. When do the rockets fire up?
   Ⓐ while the orbiter is circling Earth
   Ⓑ right before landing
   Ⓒ at liftoff

3. When do the rockets run out of fuel?
   Ⓐ after two minutes
   Ⓑ after they fall from the orbiter
   Ⓒ on the runway

4. When does the orbiter enter its orbit?
   Ⓐ before dawn
   Ⓑ after the big fuel tank falls to the sea
   Ⓒ after 14 hours

5. When do the orbiter's engines slow it down?
   Ⓐ when the shuttle is ready to return to Earth
   Ⓑ before it reaches orbit
   Ⓒ at liftoff

Name _____   Date _____

≋ **Read the story.**

Black Widow Spiders

Did you know that the black widow spider is one of the most poisonous spiders in the world? But only the females can hurt you. The males are harmless. The female's poison is much stronger than that of a rattlesnake. A person who has been bitten can die if he or she does not get treatment.

The female black widow is about half an inch long. She is black and has red marks on her belly. The black widow gets her name from the fact that she sometimes eats her mate. The male is one-third of the female's size. He doesn't have any red marks.

Let's observe one black widow female. When we first see her, she is hanging upside down in her web. She stays there for three days without moving. Her skin becomes too small, so she sheds it. She grows a new, larger skin. This is called molting, and it happens about eight times during her life.

One day a male black widow comes to the edge of the female's web. He strums on the web. If the female is ready to mate, she will strum also. If not, she might chase and eat him. It is dangerous to be a male black widow.

After mating the female weaves a small, silk sac. This is where she will lay 250 to 750 eggs. Black widows lay their eggs in the spring. The female guards the egg sac for about a month. Then baby spiders, or spiderlings, hatch. The spiderlings are small and helpless when they come out of the egg sac. Many are eaten by birds or insects. Some are even eaten by their mother. Most, however, live and become adults.

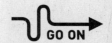

1. Put these events in the order that they happened. What happened first? Write the number **1** on the line by that sentence. Then write the number **2** by the sentence that tells what happened next. Write the number **3** by the sentence that tells what happened last.

_____ The spiderlings hatch.

_____ The female makes the egg sac.

_____ The male black widow strums on the web.

≋ **Darken the circle for the phrase that best answers each question.**

2. When does the female black widow hang in her web without moving?
   Ⓐ after eating
   Ⓑ before laying eggs
   Ⓒ while she is molting

3. When does the female black widow strum on her web?
   Ⓐ when she is ready to mate
   Ⓑ when she is hungry
   Ⓒ when she is sleepy

4. When does the female make an egg sac?
   Ⓐ when she is molting
   Ⓑ after mating
   Ⓒ before biting someone

5. When do black widows lay their eggs?
   Ⓐ in the spring
   Ⓑ during summer
   Ⓒ before the first snow

Name _____   Date _____

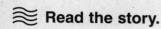

≋ **Read the story.**

Mary McLeod Bethune

Today almost all children in the United States go to school. But this was not always true. In the 1880s, there were few schools for African Americans. This was the case in South Carolina, where Mary McLeod lived.

Mary McLeod was one of 17 children. Her whole family had to work hard to make ends meet. Mary picked cotton in the fields. But she dreamed of learning to read. When she was nine, her dream came true. A church opened a school. Mr. McLeod could spare only one child. He sent Mary. Mary studied hard for the next three years. She loved school.

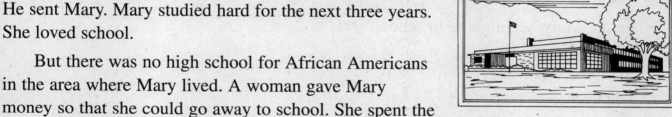

But there was no high school for African Americans in the area where Mary lived. A woman gave Mary money so that she could go away to school. She spent the next seven years in Scotia, a school in North Carolina. She graduated in 1894. Mary spent the rest of her life giving back the gift of education she had received. She taught in small towns for eight years. During this time she met and married Albertus Bethune.

Mary loved teaching. But she dreamed of having her own school. In 1904 she moved to Florida. There she opened a school for girls. In two years she had two hundred and fifty girls and four teachers. It was hard to keep the school open. There were never enough funds.

In 1923 Mary's school joined with a boys' school. Its new name was Bethune-Cookman College. Mary was the president of this school until 1942. She became known as a leader and received many awards. From 1935 to 1944, she served as an advisor to President Roosevelt.

GO ON

1. Put these events in the order that they happened. What happened first? Write the number **1** on the line by that sentence. Then write the number **2** by the sentence that tells what happened next. Write the number **3** by the sentence that tells what happened last.

_____ Mary's school joined with a boys' school.

_____ Mary picked cotton in the fields.

_____ Mary married Albertus Bethune.

≈ **Darken the circle for the phrase that best answers each question.**

2. When did Mary begin going to school?
   Ⓐ before she was six
   Ⓑ after she was twelve
   Ⓒ when she was nine

3. When did Mary graduate from Scotia?
   Ⓐ in 1894
   Ⓑ when she was 12
   Ⓒ in May 1898

4. When did Mary open her own school?
   Ⓐ before she got married
   Ⓑ after she moved to Florida
   Ⓒ when she lived in North Carolina

5. When did Mary serve as an advisor to President Roosevelt?
   Ⓐ from 1935 to 1944
   Ⓑ when she was 35
   Ⓒ when she graduated from Scotia

44

Lesson 7

≋ **Read the story.**

Conjunto Music

There are many kinds of music. One kind is called conjunto. Flaco Jiménez says his family started it.

Flaco's grandfather went to dances in New Braunfels. That's a town in Texas settled long ago by German people. They danced to German tunes called polkas. Flaco's grandfather watched how the tunes were played. Then he bought an accordion. An accordion is an instrument shaped like a box. He learned how to play polkas. Flaco's father grew up with that sound. In the 1930s, he learned to play polkas as well.

In time Flaco's father mixed Mexican folk songs with the German dance tunes. The new sound was soon called conjunto. Flaco's father made up new songs to go with the beat. As Flaco grew up, he learned to play the tunes.

A conjunto group uses an accordion, a guitar, a bass, and drums. Flaco plays the accordion and sings. He's mixed in a bit of American jazz. Flaco and his band play around the world. They have won many awards. Their lively beat makes people want to dance.

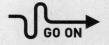

1. Put these events in the order that they happened. What happened first? Write the number **1** on the line by that sentence. Then write the number **2** by the sentence that tells what happened next. Write the number **3** by the sentence that tells what happened last.

    _____ Flaco's grandfather went to German dances.

    _____ Flaco learned to play conjunto music.

    _____ Flaco's father mixed Mexican and German tunes.

≋ **Darken the circle for the phrase that best answers each question.**

2. Who was the first Jiménez to play the accordion?
    Ⓐ Flaco
    Ⓑ Flaco's father
    Ⓒ Flaco's grandfather

3. What kind of music started the conjunto style?
    Ⓐ polka music
    Ⓑ drum beats
    Ⓒ American jazz

4. What did Flaco's father do after his music was called conjunto?
    Ⓐ learned to play polkas
    Ⓑ made up new songs
    Ⓒ mixed Mexican and German tunes

5. When did Flaco's father learn to play polkas?
    Ⓐ after Flaco's grandfather bought an accordion
    Ⓑ after Flaco and his band won awards
    Ⓒ after Flaco and his band played around the world

Lesson 8

≋ **Read the story.**

Dogs That Guide

In 1918 a doctor and his pet dog walked with a soldier who was blind. They were outside a German hospital. The doctor had to go in the building for a short time. The soldier and dog waited outside. When the doctor came out, the soldier and dog weren't there.

The doctor looked all around. He found them on the other side of the hospital yard. The doctor saw that his pet had led the soldier there safely. He thought a trained dog might be able to do more. So he taught a dog to lead a person. It worked out well. The German government helped start a program to teach dogs to be guides.

Dorothy Eustis went to Germany to find out about the guide dog course. When she came back to the United States, she wrote about it for a magazine. Soon more people knew of the guide dogs.

The best dogs for the job are smart and fit. They behave well and make good choices. It takes more than two years to train a puppy to be a guide dog. When the dog is fourteen months old, it learns to be a guide dog. It learns to know right and left. It learns when to cross a busy street and when it is not safe to cross. A dog is trained for months. Then the owner and the dog meet, and they practice for four months.

The first United States school for guide dogs opened in 1929. Now there are many schools, and there are more than 6,000 people with guide dogs.

1. Put these events in the order that they happened. What happened first? Write the number **1** on the line by that sentence. Then write the number **2** by the sentence that tells what happened next. Write the number **3** by the sentence that tells what happened last.

   _____ The doctor saw the soldier and dog on the other side of the yard.

   _____ The doctor taught a dog to lead a person.

   _____ The doctor couldn't find the soldier and dog.

≋ **Darken the circle for the phrase that best answers each question.**

2. When did the doctor go in the building?
   Ⓐ after he walked with the soldier
   Ⓑ after he looked all around
   Ⓒ after he found his pet dog

3. What did Eustis do after she returned from Germany?
   Ⓐ found out about a guide dog course
   Ⓑ trained a dog
   Ⓒ wrote about the guide dog course

4. When did the German government start a program to teach dogs to be guides?
   Ⓐ after Eustis went to Germany
   Ⓑ after the United States opened a guide dog school
   Ⓒ after the doctor taught a dog to lead a person

5. When was the first guide dog school started in the United States?
   Ⓐ 1981
   Ⓑ 1929
   Ⓒ 1918

Name _____   Date _____

Writing

≈ **Read the story. Think about the sequence, or time order. Then answer the questions in complete sentences.**

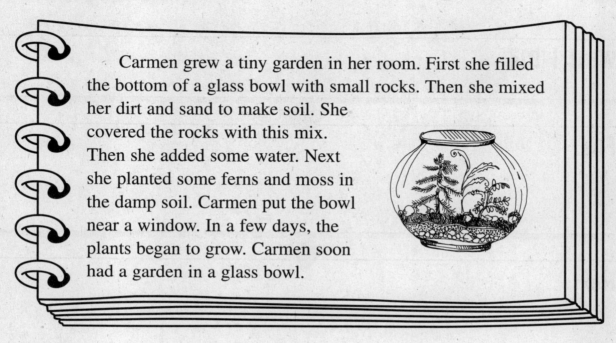

Carmen grew a tiny garden in her room. First she filled the bottom of a glass bowl with small rocks. Then she mixed her dirt and sand to make soil. She covered the rocks with this mix. Then she added some water. Next she planted some ferns and moss in the damp soil. Carmen put the bowl near a window. In a few days, the plants began to grow. Carmen soon had a garden in a glass bowl.

1. When did Carmen mix dirt and sand?

_____

_____

2. When did Carmen add water?

_____

_____

3. When did Carmen put the bowl near a window?

_____

_____

4. When did the plants begin to grow?

_____

_____

GO ON →

Prewriting

≋ Think about something that you have done, such as dressing to go out in cold weather, planning a party, or going to see a movie. Write the events in sequence below.

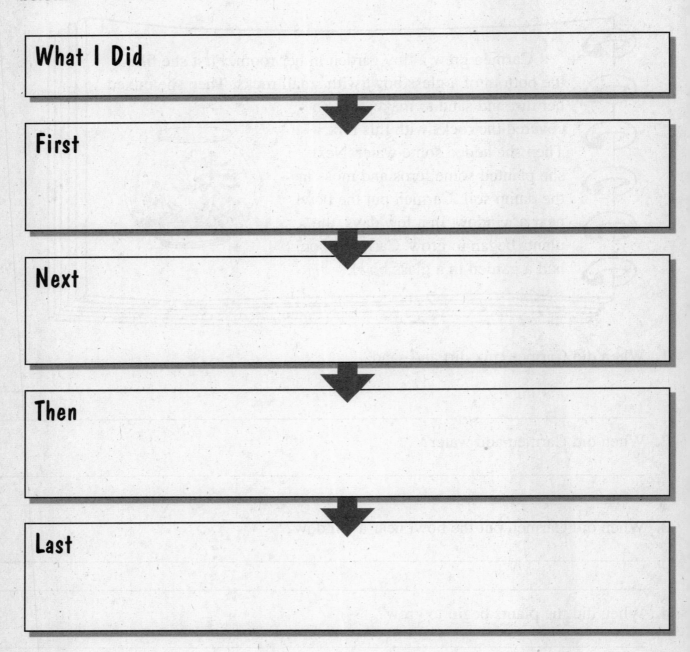

What I Did

First

Next

Then

Last

On Your Own

≋ Now use another sheet of paper to write a story about what you have done. Write the events in the order that they happened. Use time order words.

Exploring Comprehension Skills 4, SV 9781419030925

Name _____ Date _____

What Is Context?

Context means all the words in a sentence or all the sentences in a paragraph. If you find a word you do not know, look at the words around it. These other words can help you figure out what the word means.

Try It!

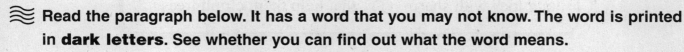 Read the paragraph below. It has a word that you may not know. The word is printed in **dark letters**. See whether you can find out what the word means.

> Treena's best friend gave her a present. It looked like a book on the outside. But the pages were blank. It was a **diary**. Treena liked the idea of making her own book. She writes in it every day. She writes about her family and friends. She writes about training her dog.

If you don't know what **diary** means, look at the context. This paragraph contains these words.

Clue: looked like a book on the outside

Clue: the pages were blank

Clue: Treena liked the idea of making her own book.

Find these clues in the paragraph. Draw a circle around them. What words do you think of when you read the clues? Write the words below.

_____

_____

Did you write *journal*? The context clue words tell you that a **diary** is a journal or record of what you do every day.

GO ON

Working with Context

This unit asks questions that you can answer by using context clues in paragraphs. There are two kinds of paragraphs. The paragraphs in the first part of this unit have blank spaces in them. You can use the context clues in the paragraphs to decide which words should go in each space. Here is an example:

> Animals have different kinds of feet. Squirrels have long toes with sharp __(1)__ that help them climb trees.

1. Ⓐ fingers   Ⓑ claws   Ⓒ gloves   Ⓓ knives

Look at the answer choices for exercise 1. Treat the paragraph as a puzzle. Which pieces don't fit? Which piece fits best? Try putting each word in the blank. See which one makes the most sense. Squirrels don't have sharp fingers or gloves or knives. *Claws* (answer **B**) is the only choice that makes sense.

~~~~~~

The paragraphs in the second part of this book are different. For these you figure out the meaning of a word that is printed in **dark letters** in the paragraph. Here is an example:

> The Inuit people use **kayaks** to travel the icy waters where they live. Kayaks are like canoes, but they have room for only one person.

The word in dark type is **kayaks**. Find the context clues. Write them below.

_____

The context clues are *travel*, *waters*, and *canoes*. Think: what are like canoes that you use to travel on water?

Now choose a word that means the same as **kayaks**.

2. In this paragraph, the word **kayaks** means
    Ⓐ sleds.   Ⓑ skis.   Ⓒ boats.   Ⓓ planes.

The context clues tell you that a kayak is a kind of boat. The correct answer is **C**.

Name _____ Date _____

≋ **Darken the circle for the word that best completes each sentence.**

People who like to __(1)__ caves are called spelunkers. To become a spelunker, it is best to begin going with __(2)__ . They take people safely through caves.

1. Ⓐ take   Ⓑ spin   Ⓒ explore   Ⓓ decide

2. Ⓐ noises   Ⓑ surprises   Ⓒ storms   Ⓓ guides

The people of South America built beautiful homes 1,900 years ago. Their homes were made of stone. The kitchen was in a __(3)__ building. In the sleeping __(4)__ , the beds were built into a wall.

3. Ⓐ mad   Ⓑ separate   Ⓒ polite   Ⓓ fast

4. Ⓐ fish   Ⓑ prairie   Ⓒ chamber   Ⓓ farm

Jim Sundberg's bat went whack! The ball flew high above the fielder's glove. It was a home run. Later, people measured the baseball __(5)__ . Someone had drawn the lines wrong. If the lines had been drawn __(6)__ , the hit would have been a foul ball, and the other team may have won.

5. Ⓐ cat   Ⓑ glove   Ⓒ diamond   Ⓓ bottom

6. Ⓐ alone   Ⓑ correctly   Ⓒ wrong   Ⓓ ugly

Saturn was named for the Roman god of farming. This great __(7)__ is famous for the rings around it. The seven main rings are made up of huge __(8)__ of ice.

7. Ⓐ planet   Ⓑ mud   Ⓒ club   Ⓓ pond

8. Ⓐ maps   Ⓑ drinks   Ⓒ chunks   Ⓓ tubs

     Exploring Comprehension Skills 4, SV 9781419030925

Name _____   Date _____

Lesson 2

≋ **Darken the circle for the word that best completes each sentence.**

Totem poles are tall wooden poles with animals painted on them. The animals look __(1)__. Parts of them look like people. One part of each animal sticks out. Bears have huge claws. Beavers have long front teeth. Crows have long, straight __(2)__.

1. Ⓐ better   Ⓑ unreal   Ⓒ orange   Ⓓ unhappy

2. Ⓐ noses   Ⓑ arms   Ⓒ buttons   Ⓓ beaks

The first Ferris wheel was taller than a twenty-story building. George Ferris made the giant wheel ride for the 1893 World's Fair. It had 36 cars. It held many __(3)__. At the top of the wheel, everyone could see for __(4)__.

3. Ⓐ passengers   Ⓑ puppets   Ⓒ rulers   Ⓓ balls

4. Ⓐ glasses   Ⓑ animals   Ⓒ miles   Ⓓ hours

The numbat has sharp claws on its front feet. The numbat uses these to tear open __(5)__ logs. Then it puts its long, sticky __(6)__ inside to catch termites. A numbat eats only termites.

5. Ⓐ yellow   Ⓑ square   Ⓒ red   Ⓓ rotten

6. Ⓐ brain   Ⓑ tongue   Ⓒ fin   Ⓓ eye

There is gold in ocean water. The __(7)__ is getting it out. Since the gold there is __(8)__, taking it out of the ocean costs a lot of money. Maybe one day someone will find an easy way to do it.

7. Ⓐ bank   Ⓑ team   Ⓒ number   Ⓓ problem

8. Ⓐ scarce   Ⓑ light   Ⓒ free   Ⓓ nickel

Lesson 3

≈ **Darken the circle for the word that best completes each sentence.**

Harriet Tubman was a slave who escaped to __(1)__ in the North. She worried about the slaves still in the South, so she returned many times. Each time, she helped slaves escape. A huge __(2)__ was offered to anyone who caught her. But no one ever did.

1. Ⓐ nowhere   Ⓑ rains   Ⓒ us   Ⓓ freedom

2. Ⓐ reward   Ⓑ trunk   Ⓒ cave   Ⓓ seal

In the spring some fish leave the __(3)__ where they live. They swim __(4)__ in rivers to ponds where they were born. These fish can find their way even when their eyes are covered. But they get lost if their noses are covered. The fish use their noses to find their way!

3. Ⓐ ocean   Ⓑ valley   Ⓒ basket   Ⓓ leaf

4. Ⓐ everywhere   Ⓑ hardly   Ⓒ upstream   Ⓓ here

Puffins are birds that live on northern coasts. __(5)__ of puffins stay at sea most of the time. They swim and dive to catch fish. They come on land to nest on high __(6)__.

5. Ⓐ Pans   Ⓑ Friends   Ⓒ Flocks   Ⓓ Barns

6. Ⓐ cliffs   Ⓑ seas   Ⓒ nets   Ⓓ pits

Smog is usually a mix of smoke and fog. It can also come from the sun acting on __(7)__ in the air. Smog can __(8)__ a person's health and kill plant life. Smog can be very thick, making it hard to see things.

7. Ⓐ stars   Ⓑ fumes   Ⓒ pals   Ⓓ pens

8. Ⓐ fix   Ⓑ save   Ⓒ give   Ⓓ damage

Name _____ Date _____

Lesson 4

≋ **Darken the circle for the word that best completes each sentence.**

A magnet can be a piece of stone or metal. Magnets come in a __(1)__ of shapes and sizes. They also come in different __(2)__, so some are weaker than others.

1. Ⓐ sack   Ⓑ box   Ⓒ variety   Ⓓ cap

2. Ⓐ zoos   Ⓑ strengths   Ⓒ rugs   Ⓓ letters

Part of Australia is a huge __(3)__. People there live hundreds of miles apart. When someone got sick in the past, doctors were too far away to help. Then a group called the Flying Doctors got together. They wanted to __(4)__ sick people. Now doctors use radios for talking to people in need. The doctors use planes to take people to the hospital.

3. Ⓐ water   Ⓑ pan   Ⓒ desert   Ⓓ street

4. Ⓐ assist   Ⓑ meet   Ⓒ forget   Ⓓ splash

Many people think we'll live in space one day. Cities will be built inside big glass bubbles. We'll ride in __(5)__ as easily as we now ride in airplanes. Space life sounds very __(6)__!

5. Ⓐ horses   Ⓑ spaceships   Ⓒ land   Ⓓ boats

6. Ⓐ merry   Ⓑ quiet   Ⓒ exciting   Ⓓ poor

A bog starts as a lake, pond, or slow-moving stream. The water gets trapped and can't __(7)__. This leads to a __(8)__ of moss. Other plants start to die. The mosses and dead plants are a floating mat that becomes a bog.

7. Ⓐ drain   Ⓑ fall   Ⓒ care   Ⓓ pay

8. Ⓐ color   Ⓑ growth   Ⓒ pot   Ⓓ fence

Exploring Comprehension Skills 4, SV 9781419030925

Name _____ Date _____

 Darken the circle for the word that best completes each sentence.

What do you do when you spill salt? Do you throw some over your left side? Once people believed that a bad __(1)__ always stared over their left side. People were afraid that spilling salt would bring bad luck. So they threw the salt over their left side. And that is how this __(2)__ began.

1. Ⓐ ten   Ⓑ card   Ⓒ spirit   Ⓓ soap

2. Ⓐ fence   Ⓑ custom   Ⓒ drink   Ⓓ sand

In the 1920s, cars were used more and more. They were also starting to go fast. And that meant __(3)__! Garrett Morgan made a machine that told drivers when to stop and go. It had __(4)__ red, green, and yellow lights.

3. Ⓐ accidents   Ⓑ nests   Ⓒ sets   Ⓓ pins

4. Ⓐ popping   Ⓑ flashing   Ⓒ eating   Ⓓ singing

A fawn lies hidden on the ground in the forest. Its spotted coat helps it stay hidden in the __(5)__ leaves. The fawn will stay very __(6)__ and quiet so it can't be heard by other animals.

5. Ⓐ fallen   Ⓑ burning   Ⓒ last   Ⓓ thin

6. Ⓐ lean   Ⓑ calm   Ⓒ sick   Ⓓ loud

Moths are insects with wings. There are many kinds of moths. They live just about everywhere. Moths are a lot like butterflies. It is often __(7)__ to tell them apart. Like butterflies, moths were once __(8)__.

7. Ⓐ usual   Ⓑ picky   Ⓒ difficult   Ⓓ tired

8. Ⓐ rats   Ⓑ hens   Ⓒ pets   Ⓓ caterpillars

57

Lesson 6

≈ **Darken the circle for the word that best completes each sentence.**

You might think of beavers as the __(1)__ of the animal world.
Beavers have strong front teeth. They cut down many trees.
Beavers use the branches to build __(2)__ for homes in the water.
They use the bark for food.

1. Ⓐ keepers   Ⓑ lumberjacks   Ⓒ pilots   Ⓓ knights

2. Ⓐ lodges   Ⓑ pillows   Ⓒ motors   Ⓓ porches

The elf owl is most often found in dry areas of the country. It sits still in its nest
during the day. Then the owl flies out to feed at __(3)__. It uses its __(4)__ senses to
find food.

3. Ⓐ market   Ⓑ sundown   Ⓒ breakfast   Ⓓ feather

4. Ⓐ flat   Ⓑ outside   Ⓒ fat   Ⓓ keen

BOLD is a group that helps blind people learn to ski. The helpers tell how the
ski trail looks. They follow the skiers. They say when to turn. They teach other skiing
__(5)__. The blind people ski on the same trails as __(6)__ else.

5. Ⓐ skills   Ⓑ fiddles   Ⓒ hairs   Ⓓ stairs

6. Ⓐ all   Ⓑ somebody   Ⓒ everyone   Ⓓ someone

The king or queen of England owns the crown jewels. These __(7)__ include
crowns, rings, bracelets, __(8)__, and swords. They are kept safe in the Tower
of London.

7. Ⓐ treasures   Ⓑ monkeys   Ⓒ carts   Ⓓ trails

8. Ⓐ tribes   Ⓑ doors   Ⓒ thoughts   Ⓓ necklaces

Name _____ Date _____

≈ **Darken the circle for the word that best completes each sentence.**

The Mummer's Parade is on New Year's Day in Philadelphia. Thousands of people __(1)__ in the parade. They dress in __(2)__ clothes. Bands play merry songs. People dance down the street. The parade lasts all day long.

1. Ⓐ visit   Ⓑ march   Ⓒ guess   Ⓓ faint

2. Ⓐ wild   Ⓑ hard   Ⓒ curly   Ⓓ wet

The first string of Christmas tree lights was made about one hundred years ago. It was made by hand. The lights all __(3)__ on and off. Soon the idea caught on. Many people wanted the lights. So some __(4)__ started to make them.

3. Ⓐ heard   Ⓑ hopped   Ⓒ winked   Ⓓ felt

4. Ⓐ lights   Ⓑ spiders   Ⓒ companies   Ⓓ plugs

The queen of England has a doll house. But it is more like a doll __(5)__! It has running water. The lights can be turned off and on. The elevator works. The piano plays __(6)__. The doll house would be great for a queen who was five inches tall!

5. Ⓐ face   Ⓑ castle   Ⓒ shoe   Ⓓ baby

6. Ⓐ ball   Ⓑ games   Ⓒ pool   Ⓓ music

Pablo Picasso was a busy __(7)__. First he learned about art from his father. Then he began painting when he was nine years old. When Pablo was thirteen, he started to study at an important art school. In his life, he did thousands of __(8)__ and paintings. He was still working when he died at age ninety-three.

7. Ⓐ girl   Ⓑ driver   Ⓒ singer   Ⓓ artist

8. Ⓐ places   Ⓑ drawings   Ⓒ chairs   Ⓓ ideas

Exploring Comprehension Skills 4, SV 9781419030925

Name _____ Date _____

≋ **Darken the circle for the word that best completes each sentence.**

A man used an airplane to cover his gas (1) . He hoped people would then stop to buy gas. He bought a B-17 airplane. It took three big machines to (2) the plane onto poles. Then he put lights under the wings. People could look up at the plane while they filled up.

1. Ⓐ well   Ⓑ hole   Ⓒ tank   Ⓓ station

2. Ⓐ fly   Ⓑ elevate   Ⓒ begin   Ⓓ drive

Turtles (3) to be very slow animals. But many turtles are really very (4) . Sea turtles can swim quickly. The green turtle can swim as fast as 20 miles per hour for a short time.

3. Ⓐ appear   Ⓑ alarm   Ⓒ nibble   Ⓓ hide

4. Ⓐ young   Ⓑ huge   Ⓒ plain   Ⓓ speedy

Some people think Lincoln wrote the Gettysburg Address on a (5) of paper. This is (6) . He wrote it carefully on a whole sheet of paper. He changed the words four times. Every time he changed the words, he copied it over again.

5. Ⓐ letter   Ⓑ scrap   Ⓒ ship   Ⓓ chain

6. Ⓐ incorrect   Ⓑ sad   Ⓒ large   Ⓓ useful

The moray eel lives in warm ocean waters. It is a strong fish with very sharp teeth. The eel hides in a hole or cave. It can catch fish with (7) speed. The moray eel will not (8) out from its hole to look for food until it is night.

7. Ⓐ brave   Ⓑ dry   Ⓒ lightning   Ⓓ half

8. Ⓐ blink   Ⓑ venture   Ⓒ list   Ⓓ roll

Lesson 9

≋ **Darken the circle for the word that best completes each sentence.**

The ends of our fingers are covered with special lines. The lines are fingerprints. Fingerprints are like rubber **soles** on shoes. The rubber bumps on shoes keep us from falling down. The lines on our fingers help us hold things.

1. In this story, the word **soles** means
Ⓐ checks. Ⓒ bottoms.
Ⓑ repairs. Ⓓ pockets.

At first only men could dance on stage. One night a man could not dance. Marie Camargo got on stage and did the man's dance. The people who were watching were **thrilled**. When Camargo finished, they clapped and threw flowers on the stage. Now many stage dancers are women.

2. In this story, the word **thrilled** means
Ⓐ delighted. Ⓒ awakened.
Ⓑ upset. Ⓓ broken.

Lodestone is a natural magnet. Long ago, sailors used a piece of lodestone to tell which direction they were going. They tied the stone to a string. They **suspended** the stone in the air. It always pointed to the north.

3. In this story, the word **suspended** means
Ⓐ crept. Ⓒ judged.
Ⓑ hung. Ⓓ grew.

The toucan is a brightly colored bird. It makes its home in the Amazon forests. During the day it flies around looking for food. At night it **roosts** in a tree.

4. In this story, the word **roosts** means
Ⓐ attacks. Ⓒ trusts.
Ⓑ wastes. Ⓓ rests.

Lesson 10

≋ **Darken the circle for the word or phrase that best completes each sentence.**

Lana was watching her favorite show on television. Her mother came into the room. "You have been watching TV since you came home from school," Mrs. Washington said. "It is becoming a bad **habit**, Lana." She turned off the program and told Lana to go outside to play.

1. In this story, the word **habit** means
   Ⓐ show.   Ⓒ way.
   Ⓑ mother.   Ⓓ day.

Fireflies aren't flies at all. They are beetles. These bugs can light up their bodies. The light **flickers** off and on. The flashing light signals other fireflies.

2. In this story, the word **flickers** means
   Ⓐ swims.   Ⓒ shadows.
   Ⓑ laughs.   Ⓓ shines.

The Ringling brothers started a very small circus. At first they did everything themselves. They made tents. They set up the circus acts. This **tough** life helped them become very famous. Now their "Greatest Show on Earth" goes all over the country.

3. In this story, the word **tough** means
   Ⓐ slow.   Ⓒ old.
   Ⓑ hard.   Ⓓ hungry.

The stingray uses its long tail to protect itself. On its tail is a sharp, poison hook. The hook can **pierce** an attacker's skin.

4. In this story, the word **pierce** means
   Ⓐ change into.   Ⓒ go through.
   Ⓑ look around.   Ⓓ stay beside.

Name _____ Date _____

≈ **Darken the circle for the word that best completes each sentence.**

The roadrunner is a bird. It is one of the fastest hunters in the desert. It can run up to twenty miles an hour. It moves so fast that it can kill a snake. The roadrunner's long legs also help it **flee** from its enemies.

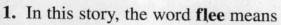

1. In this story, the word **flee** means
   - Ⓐ want.
   - Ⓒ run.
   - Ⓑ know.
   - Ⓓ set.

A man had been in jail for most of his life. He decided to make a garden. He planted seeds and watered them. As the plants grew, he began to change. He changed from a **bitter** man to a very peaceful man. He said that working in the garden made him feel free.

2. In this story, the word **bitter** means
   - Ⓐ jolly.
   - Ⓒ steady.
   - Ⓑ angry.
   - Ⓓ healthy.

The skunk has a special way to protect itself. It sprays its enemies with a liquid from under its tail. This liquid has a **foul** smell. So the skunk is left alone.

3. In this story, the word **foul** means
   - Ⓐ great.
   - Ⓒ cloudy.
   - Ⓑ dandy.
   - Ⓓ terrible.

The leek is a plant like the onion. The people of Wales **respect** the leek. Long ago it helped them fight a war. They could not tell who was on their side. So the people from Wales put leeks in their caps.

4. In this story, the word **respect** means
   - Ⓐ like.
   - Ⓒ build.
   - Ⓑ melt.
   - Ⓓ turn.

63

Name _____ Date _____

≈ **Darken the circle for the word or phrase that best completes each sentence.**

Catnip is a plant. It belongs to the mint family. It grows wild along many roads. Cats love to roll and play in catnip. They also like to eat it. They like the **taste** of the plant.

1. In this story, the word **taste** means
   - Ⓐ fear.
   - Ⓑ dash.
   - Ⓒ flavor.
   - Ⓓ example.

In 1888 there was a terrible **blizzard** in New York City. It lasted for three days. There were strong winds. Blowing snow was all that could be seen. Many people died in this storm.

2. In this story, the word **blizzard** means
   - Ⓐ house.
   - Ⓑ rain.
   - Ⓒ guard.
   - Ⓓ snowstorm.

People have **measured** time in many ways. At first, people used the sun, moon, and stars to tell time. Now we use clocks to keep track of time.

3. In this story, the word **measured** means
   - Ⓐ closed.
   - Ⓑ opened.
   - Ⓒ found the length of.
   - Ⓓ put in a bottle.

The glass snake is not a snake at all. It is a lizard without legs. Its tail is twice the length of its body. The glass snake can **shed** its tail if it is attacked. A new tail will grow in its place.

4. In this story, the word **shed** means
   - Ⓐ fool.
   - Ⓑ lose.
   - Ⓒ puff up.
   - Ⓓ take in.

64

Name _____ Date _____

≋ **Darken the circle for the word that best completes each sentence.**

Piranhas are fish. They live in South American rivers. These fish tend to swim in large groups. They will tear the flesh off an animal or person that gets in the water. In just minutes, all that is left is the **skeleton**.

1. In this story, the word **skeleton** means
   - Ⓐ key.
   - Ⓒ butter.
   - Ⓑ pie.
   - Ⓓ bones.

A cartoon is a **humorous** way to tell a story or make a point. A cartoon can be one drawing or a set of drawings. A cartoon may have words with the picture. But words aren't always needed.

2. In this story, the word **humorous** means
   - Ⓐ cozy.
   - Ⓒ dangerous.
   - Ⓑ funny.
   - Ⓓ thirsty.

Pluto is the planet farthest from the sun. Not much is known about this **distant** planet. It is quite cold there since it is so far from the sun. Scientists don't think that there is any life on Pluto.

3. In this story, the word **distant** means
   - Ⓐ faraway.
   - Ⓒ lucky.
   - Ⓑ nearby.
   - Ⓓ pleasant.

Long ago, **vessels** crossed the water from northern Europe to other countries. They carried Viking warriors. At first the Vikings fought with people. Then the Vikings decided to trade. They set up many new trade centers.

4. In this story, the word **vessels** means
   - Ⓐ whales.
   - Ⓒ ships.
   - Ⓑ bottles.
   - Ⓓ horses.

Name _____ Date _____

Lesson 14

≋ **Darken the circle for the word that best completes each sentence.**

Wildflowers grow in many **environments**. Some are found in woods or fields. Others grow on mountains or in streams and ponds. Wildflowers can grow in the desert, too.

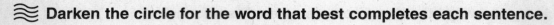

1. In this story, the word **environments** means
   Ⓐ blossoms.   Ⓒ oceans.
   Ⓑ settings.   Ⓓ insects.

Some Americans want to help others. They join the Peace Corps. These workers go to other nations. They try to **educate** the people to help themselves.

2. In this story, the word **educate** means
   Ⓐ present.   Ⓒ hurry.
   Ⓑ bounce.   Ⓓ teach.

At one time, women could not vote or own land. Susan B. Anthony knew that women didn't have the same rights as men. She worked hard to **obtain** equal rights for women. But it was not until many years after her death that women finally won these rights.

3. In this story, the word **obtain** means
   Ⓐ follow.   Ⓒ get.
   Ⓑ notice.   Ⓓ move.

Sometimes a huge **mass** of ice breaks off from a glacier. It falls into the sea and floats. This block of ice is called an iceberg. Ships must be careful of icebergs.

4. In this story, the word **mass** means
   Ⓐ shade.   Ⓒ block.
   Ⓑ tooth.   Ⓓ church.

Exploring Comprehension Skills 4, SV 9781419030925

Name _____ Date _____

Lesson 15

≋ **Darken the circle for the word or phrase that best completes each sentence.**

Running is fun. Some people like to run against each other. But most people **prefer** to run against themselves. They may try to run more and more miles each day, or they may try to run for longer and longer times.

1. In this story, the word **prefer** means
   Ⓐ help.   Ⓒ measure.
   Ⓑ shop   Ⓓ like.

Many animals live in shell houses, but they get their shells in different ways. A turtle's shell is really part of its skeleton. It wears its bones on the outside. A **clam** has no bones. It makes its shell from salt in the ocean.

2. In this story, the word **clam** means
   Ⓐ shark.   Ⓒ small land animal.
   Ⓑ fish.   Ⓓ kind of sea animal.

Babe Ruth was the home-run king for a long time. He hit a record 714 home runs. Ruth played his last game in 1935. Then he **retired**. It took almost forty years for someone to break his record.

3. In this story, the word **retired** means
   Ⓐ quit work.   Ⓒ went to sleep.
   Ⓑ played songs.   Ⓓ forgot something.

There are giant ships more than seven hundred feet long. These ships were built to carry tons of wheat from place to place. They have a road folded up in back. When they get to shore, the road unfolds. The **cargo** is moved on and off.

4. In this story, the word **cargo** means
   Ⓐ truck.   Ⓒ load.
   Ⓑ garbage.   Ⓓ flower.

Name _____ Date _____

≈ **Darken the circle for the word that best completes each sentence.**

When you leave your house in the morning, it doesn't just stay the same. Sunlight falls on the rug. It warms the **fibers**, making them wave slowly. This waving warms the air and moves it around.

1. In this story, the word **fibers** means
- Ⓐ threads.
- Ⓒ rooms.
- Ⓑ desks.
- Ⓓ walls.

The poison arrow frog is found in South America. It has **vivid** colors on its skin. The frog's colorful skin warns birds not to eat it.

2. In this story, the word **vivid** means
- Ⓐ bright.
- Ⓒ rotten.
- Ⓑ dull.
- Ⓓ painful.

The America's Cup is a boat race. It first started more than one hundred years ago. Boat builders in the United States had built a boat that they thought was much faster than the old kind. They sailed it across the sea and **challenged** the people there to a race. The new boat did win! The prize was a silver cup.

3. In this story, the word **challenged** means
- Ⓐ dared.
- Ⓒ hurried.
- Ⓑ cooked.
- Ⓓ caged.

Your body makes its own medicine. When you are **alarmed**, your body makes something that helps you run from trouble. When you are hurt, your body makes something that helps you heal.

4. In this story, the word **alarmed** means
- Ⓐ happy.
- Ⓒ scared.
- Ⓑ tall.
- Ⓓ cold.

Name _____   Date _____

Writing

≋ **Read each story. Write a word on each line that makes sense in the story.**

Sara got out the water hose and bucket and gave her dog Dusty a bath. Dusty did not like to be

(1) _____. As soon as his bath was

over, he rolled in the **(2)** _____.

Our family likes to
go camping. It's fun to sit
outside the tent at night
and look up at the

(3) _____.

I wish we could go camping every **(4)** _____

A new boy came to our **(5)** _____

today. We wanted to be friendly, so we asked him to

(6) _____ with us.

⌐⌐ GO ON

Name _____ Date _____

Prewriting

≋ Look through a book. Find a word that you do not know. Write the word on the chart.
Write the sentence that you found. Then complete the rest of the chart.

Word	Sentence
_____	_____ _____ _____ _____
What I think the word means	**The definition I found**
_____ _____ _____ _____ _____ _____ _____	_____ _____ _____ _____ _____ _____ _____

On Your Own

≋ Now use another sheet of paper. Write a short paragraph that uses the new word.
Be sure to include clues that give a hint about the meaning of the word.

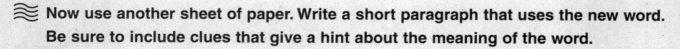

Exploring Comprehension Skills 4, SV 9781419030925

Unit 4

What Is a Main Idea?

The main idea of a story tells what it is about. The other sentences add details to the main idea. Often the main idea is stated in the first or last sentence of the paragraph. Sometimes you may find the main idea in the middle of the paragraph.

This example may help you think about main ideas:

$$5 \quad + \quad 6 \quad + \quad 7 \quad = \quad 18$$
$$\text{detail} + \text{detail} + \text{detail} = \text{main idea}$$

The *5*, *6*, and *7* are like details. They are smaller than their sum, *18*. The *18*, like the main idea, is bigger. It is made of several smaller parts.

Try It!

≋ **Read the story below. Draw a line under the main idea.**

> Jupiter is the biggest planet in the solar system. Jupiter is 88,600 miles in diameter. That is 11 times the diameter of Earth. Jupiter is so big that over 1,300 Earths could fit inside it.

The main idea sentence is the first sentence in the story. All the other sentences are details. They give more facts about Jupiter.

The main idea could come at the end of the story:

> Jupiter is 88,600 miles in diameter. That is 11 times the diameter of Earth. Jupiter is so big that over 1,300 Earths could fit inside it. Jupiter is the biggest planet in the solar system.

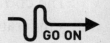
GO ON

Practice Finding the Main Idea

This unit asks you to find main ideas. Read the story and answer the question below. Darken the circle by the correct answer.

> There are more than three thousand kinds of frogs. The grass frog is so small it can sit on an acorn. The goliath frog of West Africa is the largest frog in the world. It is the size of a cat. The water-holding frog uses the skin it has shed to make a bag around itself. This bag holds in water and keeps the frog cool.

1. The story mainly tells
   - Ⓐ about the goliath frog.
   - Ⓑ about a tiny frog.
   - Ⓒ that there are many kinds of frogs.
   - Ⓓ about the water-holding frog.

The correct answer is **C**. The story includes details about three kinds of frogs. These details support the first sentence.

Sometimes a story does not have a main idea sentence. You can figure out the main idea by reading the details. Read the story below.

> The Sahara Desert is found in North Africa. The desert gets from five to ten inches of rain a year. But sometimes there are dry periods that can last years. The temperature may reach 135 degrees during the day.

2. The story mainly tells
   - Ⓐ how hot the Sahara is.
   - Ⓑ facts about the Sahara.
   - Ⓒ where the Sahara is found.
   - Ⓓ how much rainfall the Sahara gets.

The correct answer is **B**. There are details about the Sahara's location, rainfall, and temperature. If you add these details together, you will get the main idea.

Name _____ Date _____

≋ **Read the stories. Darken the circle for the phrase that best completes each sentence.**

The mind can work very well for many years. People used to think that age slowed down the mind. But this isn't true. The mind is just like any other muscle in the body. The more you use it, the stronger it becomes. Muscles that aren't used will grow weak. Muscles that are used will stay strong. Older people who use their minds will think as well as ever.

1. The story mainly tells
   Ⓐ how using the mind keeps it strong.
   Ⓑ who has the biggest muscles in their arms.
   Ⓒ who is smarter than other people.
   Ⓓ how the mind becomes weak with age.

Horse shows are the place to see beautiful horses. The riders and horses get scores for each event. First all the riders walk their horses around the ring. Then they trot the horses, making them go faster and faster. Finally they gallop. When they jump over logs or ponds, the riders must not fall. The best riders and horses get ribbons and prizes.

2. The story mainly tells
   Ⓐ which kinds of horses jump the highest.
   Ⓑ who gets prizes for galloping.
   Ⓒ what horses and riders do in horse shows.
   Ⓓ how the horses jump fences.

Wesley was learning to sing and play the guitar. He wanted to play in the school talent show at the end of the year. His guitar teacher told him he should practice in front of family members to get used to playing in front of people. Wesley asked his grandparents if he could play for them and their friends. They said yes. Wesley played for the whole group. They clapped and cheered when he finished! Wesley felt ready to play in the talent show.

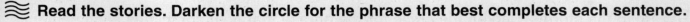

3. The story mainly tells
   Ⓐ how Wesley learned to sing.
   Ⓑ how Wesley prepared for the talent show.
   Ⓒ what kinds of songs Wesley played on the guitar.
   Ⓓ where Wesley's grandparents lived.

Lesson 2

≋ **Read the stories. Darken the circle for the phrase that best completes each sentence.**

Some butterflies lay their eggs on just one kind of plant. By tasting the plant, they know which one is right. Sometimes butterflies taste the wrong plant. So they fly to another plant and taste again. When they find the right plant, they lay their eggs there. Soon the eggs hatch. The hungry babies eat the plant their mother chose!

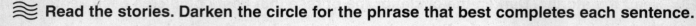

1. The story mainly tells
   Ⓐ when baby butterflies come out of eggs.
   Ⓑ how butterflies choose where to lay eggs.
   Ⓒ what flies from one plant to another.
   Ⓓ how butterflies always taste the right plant.

Kings and queens had the earliest zoos. They wanted to show off their money by keeping strange animals. Later people kept animals in zoos because they wanted to learn about them. Students could take classes at the zoo. Today zoos try to help certain animals. These animals are disappearing from their wild homes. So zoos help keep these animals safe.

2. The story mainly tells
   Ⓐ how rulers showed off their money.
   Ⓑ which people learned about zoo animals.
   Ⓒ how zoos have changed over the years.
   Ⓓ how animals will never disappear.

Years ago doctors made house calls. They took care of sick people at home. Later they stopped making house calls. They wanted people to go to hospitals instead. But hospitals cost so much money. Now some doctors have decided that the old way is better. They have found that house calls cost people less than going to the hospital.

3. The story mainly tells
   Ⓐ which sick people go to hospitals.
   Ⓑ why some doctors now go to people's houses.
   Ⓒ when doctors changed their minds.
   Ⓓ how much money doctors make today.

Name _____ Date _____

≈ **Read the stories. Darken the circle for the phrase that best completes each sentence.**

The first dollhouses were built for grown-ups. These houses were as tall as people. They were filled with pretty things. Rich people made these dollhouses look like their own homes. Only later did they build smaller dollhouses for children. Some of these are still around. They help us learn what real houses looked like long ago.

1. The story mainly tells
   Ⓐ when people made dollhouses for children.
   Ⓑ which dollhouses were the tallest.
   Ⓒ what the first dollhouses were like.
   Ⓓ which people didn't build dollhouses.

Mother ducks take baby ducks away from each other. This is the way it happens. The mother ducks take their babies swimming. Soon the pond is full of ducks. The mother ducks quack. They swim around the baby ducks. The mother duck that quacks loudest gets the greatest number of babies. Some mother ducks may have forty baby ducks. Others may have only two or three.

2. The story mainly tells
   Ⓐ which duck quacks the loudest.
   Ⓑ how mother ducks take babies away.
   Ⓒ when the ducks go swimming.
   Ⓓ how baby ducks choose their mother.

The African American man stared at the picture on the wall. It was a very old family picture. The man in the picture was a soldier. He died for his country. The eyes of the man in the picture seemed to ask, "Remember me?" But the young man thought, "No. People don't remember you." So he quit his job. He worked at passing a law that would put up a statue in Washington, D.C. The statue would honor the five thousand African Americans who died in the War for Independence.

3. The story mainly tells
   Ⓐ in which war the man in the picture died.
   Ⓑ about a statue for African Americans.
   Ⓒ who fought for our country's independence.
   Ⓓ that the statue honors only white men.

Name _____   Date _____

≋ **Read the stories. Darken the circle for the phrase that best completes each sentence.**

Miss Kitty the house cat leads a quiet life. When she is outside, she loves to lounge in the sun on the back patio. When she is inside, she sits in the window and watches the birds eating on the feeders. She only moves when she hears her owner open a can of cat food. After eating she curls up in her bed for a long nap.

1. The story mainly tells
   Ⓐ what types of birds Miss Kitty watches.
   Ⓑ why Miss Kitty watches the birds.
   Ⓒ what Miss Kitty does during the day.
   Ⓓ how Miss Kitty knows it is time to eat.

Many families in Japan collect dolls. These families have a Doll Day for Girls and a Doll Day for Boys. On the girls' day, families bring out special dolls. The dolls are dressed as old kings and queens from Japan. On the boys' day, families bring out other dolls. The dolls are dressed as famous fighters from the past. These doll days are very special to the people of Japan.

2. The story mainly tells
   Ⓐ who plays with dolls in Japan.
   Ⓑ which dolls are famous in Japan.
   Ⓒ what doll days are like in Japan.
   Ⓓ how much the famous dolls cost.

Calamity Jane was a famous woman of the Wild West. She was famous because she was so tough. She lived during the 1800s. She learned to ride a horse and shoot a gun at an early age. People could always hear her coming. She also liked dressing in men's clothes. There weren't many women like Calamity Jane.

3. The story mainly tells
   Ⓐ why Calamity Jane was famous.
   Ⓑ how Calamity Jane dressed.
   Ⓒ when Calamity Jane rode a horse.
   Ⓓ when Calamity Jane was called a coward.

76

Name _____   Date _____

Lesson 5

≋ **Read the stories. Darken the circle for the phrase that best completes each sentence.**

Children learn their first lessons in banking when they use piggy banks. Children put pennies in their banks and wait for the number of pennies to grow. The money is safe there. When the bank is full, the child can buy something with the money. In the same way, children's parents put their money in a real bank. It's safe there. They can add more money every month. Later they can use it to buy the things they need.

1. The story mainly tells

   (A) how children spend their money.
   (B) how a piggy bank is a lesson in banking.
   (C) when grown people put money in a bank.
   (D) why grown people don't use piggy banks.

Zoo elephants get very good care. Each morning zookeepers give them a special bath. They wash the elephants with water and a brush. Then they paint oil on their skin and rub oil on their feet. This is very important in elephant care. It helps the elephants feel good. When zoo visitors come to see them, the elephants are happy.

2. The story mainly tells
   (A) why zookeepers have happy lives.
   (B) who paints oil on elephants.
   (C) why zookeepers give elephants special care.
   (D) how much elephants eat.

Not long ago, people raised their own chickens. They fed the chickens leftover food. They also gathered fresh eggs every day. Every morning the roosters awakened everybody. Sometimes the family cooked a chicken for dinner. Today life has changed. Most people buy chickens and eggs at stores. They have clocks to awaken them.

3. The story mainly tells
   (A) why people once raised chickens.
   (B) why chickens give fresh eggs.
   (C) when the family cooked a chicken.
   (D) where the chicken pens were found.

Name _____   Date _____

≋ **Read the stories. Darken the circle for the phrase that best completes each sentence.**

Josie and her father were going fishing. Josie made sure her fishing pole had a hook and plenty of fishing line before she put it in the back of the truck. Josie's father packed some snacks in case they got hungry. The last thing Josie packed was a basket for holding the fish she and her father would catch.

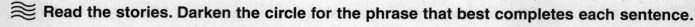

1. The story mainly tells
   Ⓐ how Josie and her father prepared for going fishing.
   Ⓑ what types of fish Josie hoped to catch.
   Ⓒ why Josie liked to go fishing.
   Ⓓ which lake had the most fish.

All winter long bears do nothing but sleep. To get ready for their winter sleep, they eat. They eat much food to get fat. The fat will become food their bodies will use while they sleep. Bears choose sleeping places such as caves. But they might also choose a hollow log or even a big pile of brush. If it gets warm on a winter day, the bear might come out to walk around. But it doesn't stay out long. Only in the spring do bears finally get up and look for food.

2. The story mainly tells
   Ⓐ what kind of life a bear leads.
   Ⓑ who likes caves for sleeping.
   Ⓒ where bears sleep in the summer.
   Ⓓ why bears love honey.

Many farmers today grow fields of yellow sunflowers. People have many uses for sunflower seeds. After the seeds are dried and salted, people buy them to eat. Some sunflower seeds are pressed to make cooking oil. Some seeds are also ground to make a kind of butter.

3. The story mainly tells
   Ⓐ why people eat salty seeds.
   Ⓑ how sunflower seeds are of great value.
   Ⓒ who uses cooking oil.
   Ⓓ who likes sunflower butter.

Lesson 7

≋ **Read the stories. Darken the circle for the phrase that best completes each sentence.**

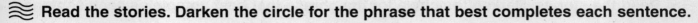

Long ago Jane Addams didn't believe that poor people were treated fairly. She wanted a law that would keep poor children from having to work. She also thought that poor women shouldn't have to work more than eight hours a day. Many of her wishes became laws.

1. The story mainly tells
  Ⓐ how Jane Addams worked to help the poor.
  Ⓑ why people are poor.
  Ⓒ when children should work long hours.
  Ⓓ how poor people were treated fairly.

Everyone knows the kind of ham people eat. But another ham is the person who runs a radio station for fun. Hams use radios to talk to other hams, even in other countries. What happens if two hams don't speak the same language? Hams have made a new language that all hams learn. It's called the Q signal language because everything starts with a *Q*. For instance, *QTH?* means "Where are you?"

2. The story mainly tells
  Ⓐ about a new language for hams everywhere.
  Ⓑ who listens to radios.
  Ⓒ about different kinds of meat.
  Ⓓ how radio hams like to eat ham.

Everything is made up of tiny things called atoms. How small are atoms? Take out a pencil. Make a tiny dot on this page. Now sharpen your pencil. Make an even smaller dot on the page. The tiniest dot that you could make would be made of millions of atoms. That's how small atoms are!

3. The story mainly tells
  Ⓐ that atoms are so small we can't even see them.
  Ⓑ where to put a dot.
  Ⓒ what a pencil is made of.
  Ⓓ how an atom is bigger than a dot.

Exploring Comprehension Skills 4, SV 9781419030925

Lesson 8

≈ **Read the stories. Darken the circle for the phrase that best completes each sentence.**

Katherine Anne Porter was born in Texas in 1890. She did not go to college, but she read many books. Porter wrote stories. But people wanted her to write a book. Her first book took twenty years to write. It was *Ship of Fools*. It was a big seller. Later it was made into a movie.

1. The story mainly tells
   - Ⓐ about Porter's first book.
   - Ⓑ that Porter was a Texan.
   - Ⓒ that Porter liked to go to the movies.
   - Ⓓ that Porter wrote many books.

Neil Armstrong was an astronaut. In 1969 he did something no one else had done before. He set foot on the moon. He said, "That's one small step for a man, one giant leap for mankind." Edwin Aldrin followed Armstrong. They placed a U.S. flag on the moon.

2. The story mainly tells
   - Ⓐ what Neil Armstrong said on the moon.
   - Ⓑ who first walked on the moon.
   - Ⓒ how Armstrong and Aldrin reached the moon.
   - Ⓓ what clothing Armstrong wore on the moon.

Earthquakes happen in places where there are great cracks in the rocks below the ground. The rocks on each side of the crack slide past each other. Suddenly the ground begins to shake. The shaking lasts for a few seconds or even minutes. Buildings sometimes fall down. The rocks settle. Then the earthquake is over.

3. The story mainly tells
   - Ⓐ what happens during an earthquake.
   - Ⓑ about the San Francisco earthquake.
   - Ⓒ what to do during an earthquake.
   - Ⓓ how to stop an earthquake.

Exploring Comprehension Skills 4, SV 9781419030925

Name _____ Date _____

Lesson 9

≋ **Read the stories. Darken the circle for the phrase that best completes each sentence.**

Two things make a tree a conifer. It must make seeds in its cones. It must also have needlelike leaves. Conifers are called evergreen trees. They look green all the time. Conifers lose and replace their leaves. But they never lose all their leaves at the same time.

1. This story mainly tells
   Ⓐ another name for the evergreen tree.
   Ⓑ about conifer trees.
   Ⓒ about different types of conifer trees.
   Ⓓ when conifer trees lose their leaves.

This book is read by sight. Braille is read by touch. Braille letters are made up of raised dots. People who are blind read by running their fingers over the letters. Braille was named after the man who invented it. Louis Braille invented Braille in 1829.

2. This story mainly tells
   Ⓐ how Louis Braille invented Braille.
   Ⓑ how to read Braille.
   Ⓒ about a special kind of writing for the blind.
   Ⓓ how to read this book.

Hair has color because it contains melanin. Dark hair has much melanin in it. Light hair has less. As people grow older, their hair has less melanin. But the hair keeps growing. So the hair looks gray or white because it doesn't have any melanin.

3. This story mainly tells
   Ⓐ how hair grows.
   Ⓑ how to change the color of hair.
   Ⓒ where melanin comes from.
   Ⓓ why hair is light or dark.

Name _____ Date _____

Lesson 10

≋ **Read the stories. Darken the circle for the phrase that best completes each sentence.**

A set is the place in which a movie is filmed. Carpenters build sets to show scenes where the action takes place. Some sets are painted to look like real rooms. They can be used for plays, films, or television shows. Sets can also be built to look like the outdoors. A set for a whole street or town can even be built.

1. The story mainly tells
   Ⓐ how television shows and movies are made.
   Ⓑ that films are made outdoors.
   Ⓒ how sets are used.
   Ⓓ that carpenters build sets.

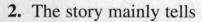

There are many Greek legends. One tells the story of Icarus, a man in prison. His father made wings of wax and feathers for him. Icarus attached the wings to his arms and was able to escape from the prison. He flew over the sea like a bird. But Icarus flew too close to the sun. The sun melted his wax wings, and Icarus fell to his death.

2. The story mainly tells
   Ⓐ about the Greek legend of Icarus.
   Ⓑ about many Greek legends.
   Ⓒ about making wings of wax.
   Ⓓ why Icarus was in prison.

When Ethel Waters was a child, she was poor. She worked as a maid for five dollars a day. Ethel knew she was talented. She began singing. She worked very hard. She sang and acted in movies and plays. In 1950 Ethel Waters won an award for acting in a play. She became known as the actress with the golden voice.

3. The story mainly tells
   Ⓐ that Ethel Waters was poor.
   Ⓑ where Ethel Waters grew up.
   Ⓒ about a famous maid.
   Ⓓ how Ethel Waters became famous.

Name _____   Date _____

≋ **Read the stories. Darken the circle for the phrase that best completes each sentence.**

Henry González wanted to run for the Texas legislature. He went to political leaders for help. They said that a Mexican American could not win. But he ran anyway. He spent $300 on his campaign. The other men who ran spent much more money. González lost the election. But he lost by only a few votes. Then González ran for city council and won. He went on to win other state and national offices.

1. The story mainly tells
   Ⓐ about a man who became a political leader.
   Ⓑ that González lived in Texas.
   Ⓒ about González's high-priced campaign.
   Ⓓ how political leaders helped González.

Dixy Lee Ray wanted to become governor. People laughed at her. There had been only four women governors in the United States. All had been elected with the help of their husbands. But Ray had never been married. She ran for governor on her own. Ray became the first woman governor of Washington.

2. The story mainly tells
   Ⓐ about the first woman governor in the United States.
   Ⓑ why Dixy Lee Ray wanted to become governor.
   Ⓒ about a woman who ran her own campaign.
   Ⓓ who Dixy Lee Ray's husband was.

Leslie woke up in a panic. Her room was dark and she was scared. She walked down the hallway to her parents' room. "Mom, I had a bad dream," Leslie said. Leslie's mother got out of bed and walked Leslie back to her room.

As she tucked Leslie in, Mom said, "It's all right. Go back to sleep." Leslie fell asleep and woke up the next morning. She had forgotten all about the bad dream.

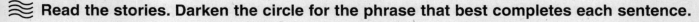

3. The story mainly tells
   Ⓐ why Leslie's mother was sleeping.
   Ⓑ what Leslie did when she had a bad dream.
   Ⓒ what Leslie dreamed about.
   Ⓓ why Leslie was scared.

Lesson 12

≋ **Read the stories. Darken the circle for the phrase that best completes each sentence.**

Anthony put down his rake and let out a sigh. The job was almost done. It had taken him all morning, but the leaves were all raked into neat piles in the yard. All Anthony had to do now was to put them in a bag. Just as Anthony got up to finish the task, the wind began to blow. Some of the leaves began to dance in the air. "Oh, no!" Anthony yelled. "Now I have to rake some more."

1. The story mainly tells
   Ⓐ when Anthony was raking leaves.
   Ⓑ how the wind blew.
   Ⓒ why Anthony raked leaves.
   Ⓓ where the leaves were.

King Louis XIV of France was a short man. He wanted to look taller. So he ordered high heels for his shoes. Then he had his shoes trimmed with lace, bows, and jewels. One pair of shoes had bows that were 16 inches wide. He had artists paint scenes on the heels of his shoes. Soon other men in France wore high-heeled shoes with flowers and bows.

2. The story mainly tells
   Ⓐ why high-heeled shoes were invented.
   Ⓑ how tall King Louis XIV was.
   Ⓒ how the king painted his heels.
   Ⓓ about shoes that men wear today.

The Loch Ness Monster has been seen many times. It lives in a lake in Scotland called Loch Ness. The waters of Loch Ness are the color of coffee. So no one has been able to take a clear picture of the monster or catch it. The monster is said to be about twenty feet long. It has a tiny head and a long neck. Its big body has flippers and many humps.

3. The story mainly tells
   Ⓐ that the monster does not exist.
   Ⓑ how many people have seen the monster.
   Ⓒ where Loch Ness is located.
   Ⓓ how no one has proved that the monster is real.

Name _____   Date _____

≋ **Read the stories. Darken the circle for the phrase that best completes each sentence.**

There were times when soldiers had no way to talk to each other. In the past, the army used pigeons to carry messages. The birds proved to be very brave. They flew through great danger. The army said carrier pigeons helped save many lives. Later some of the birds were given medals. They were real heroes.

1. The story mainly tells
   Ⓐ how pigeons carry messages.
   Ⓑ why pigeons were brave.
   Ⓒ how pigeons helped the army.
   Ⓓ how birds were given medals.

Some signs can talk! These signs are used in selling houses. As you drive by the sign, a machine on the sign sends signals to your car radio. A voice tells you how big the house is and its price. If you want to buy the house, you can stop and look at it.

2. The story mainly tells
   Ⓐ where to find big houses.
   Ⓑ how some signs can help sell houses.
   Ⓒ about the price of the house.
   Ⓓ how signals are sent to your house.

Joseph Cinque lived in West Africa. He and 52 others were captured to be slaves. They were put on a ship. One night he escaped from his chains. He and his friends took over the ship. They did not want to become slaves. They wanted to sail back to their home. But the ship was forced to land in the United States. Cinque took his case to the Supreme Court. The Court ruled that Cinque could go back home to Africa.

3. The story mainly tells
   Ⓐ about a man who fought against slavery.
   Ⓑ about a ship ride.
   Ⓒ about life as a slave.
   Ⓓ about life in West Africa.

Lesson 14

≈ **Read the stories. Darken the circle for the phrase that best completes each sentence.**

Greenland is a cold country. Most of it is covered with ice and snow. It is a white land. When explorers first found Greenland, they saw green grass. They named the place Greenland. Then they discovered that only the coast is green.

1. The story mainly tells
ⓐ what the weather is like in Greenland.
ⓑ where Greenland is located.
ⓒ how Greenland got its name.
ⓓ that Greenland is an island.

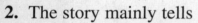

The bee hummingbird is the size of a bee. This bird is two and one-half inches long. It weighs the same as a lump of sugar. It has a long beak. This tiny bird lives in Cuba.

2. The story mainly tells
ⓐ about a kind of bee.
ⓑ how a hummingbird is like a bee.
ⓒ about the smallest insect.
ⓓ about the bee hummingbird.

Settlers nearly died trying to cross Death Valley. The valley lies in two states. It is located in California and Nevada. Death Valley is a desert. It's the hottest place in the United States. It's also the lowest point. It lies 282 feet below sea level. Settlers gave the valley its name.

3. The story mainly tells
ⓐ what life is like in Death Valley.
ⓑ how Death Valley got its name.
ⓒ how Death lies 282 feet above sea level.
ⓓ how Death Valley stretches into three states.

Name _____ Date _____

≋ **Read the stories. Darken the circle for the phrase that best completes each sentence.**

A chameleon is a kind of lizard. Its skin is clear, but it can change color. Under its skin are layers of cells. These cells have yellow, black, and red color in them. Anger makes these colors darken. Fear makes them lighten. It also makes yellow spots appear. Temperature and light can also cause these colors to change. These changes make the chameleon hard to see. Changing colors can save a chameleon's life.

1. The story mainly tells
   Ⓐ that a chameleon has clear skin.
   Ⓑ how a chameleon's skin can change color.
   Ⓒ where chameleons live.
   Ⓓ that sometimes a chameleon has yellow spots.

A family tree doesn't grow in the yard. This kind of chart shows the members of a family. Some people wonder about their roots. They like tracing their ancestors. When they chart a family tree, they can see how branches of their family formed. Sometimes exciting stories about ancestors come to light. A family tree is a lot of work, but it is great fun, too.

2. The story mainly tells
   Ⓐ what a family tree is.
   Ⓑ how people wonder about their roots.
   Ⓒ how family branches are formed.
   Ⓓ how stories about ancestors come to light.

Rice is grown in a different way from many other crops. Young rice plants are planted in flooded fields. These fields of water are called paddies. The rice plants grow in two to four inches of water. Rice has long leaves and clusters of flowers. The flowers turn into grains of rice and are collected.

3. The story mainly tells
   Ⓐ about ways to cook rice.
   Ⓑ how rice plants grow.
   Ⓒ how rice is collected.
   Ⓓ why the rice fields are flooded.

Name _____ Date _____

Lesson 16

≈ **Read the stories. Darken the circle for the phrase that best completes each sentence.**

Water has great power. Waves beat at rock shores day after day. The waves carve out caves in the rock. Underground streams flow through rock. The water slowly wears away the rock. The streams carve out underground caves.

1. The story mainly tells
   - Ⓐ where caves are found.
   - Ⓑ how tides affect caves.
   - Ⓒ how water forms caves.
   - Ⓓ how water breaks rock.

Clara Barton worked as a nurse in the Civil War. She traveled with the Union Army. After the war, she headed a search for missing soldiers. When the search ended, she went to Europe. There she worked with the European Red Cross. After she came home, she wanted to start a Red Cross in the United States. She worked very hard. Later she became president of the Red Cross. She worked with the Red Cross for 23 years.

2. The story mainly tells
   - Ⓐ where Clara Barton lived.
   - Ⓑ why Clara Barton became a nurse.
   - Ⓒ about Clara Barton's work with the Red Cross.
   - Ⓓ that Clara Barton worked in Europe.

Camels have one or two humps on their backs. The humps are made of fat. The fat stores energy. When there isn't much food, the camel lives off the energy from its humps.

3. The story mainly tells
   - Ⓐ about the humps of camels.
   - Ⓑ how many humps a camel has.
   - Ⓒ how much fat is in a camel's humps.
   - Ⓓ how heavy a camel's humps can be.

Unit 4

Writing

≋ **Read each story. Think about the main idea. Write the main idea in your own words.**

People have learned much about the oceans. They learned through exploring these huge bodies of water. Because oceans are so deep, there is much more to learn about them. There still are many questions about life in the oceans.

1. What is the main idea of this story?

_____

_____

_____

Helen Keller was blind and deaf. She could not speak as a child. But she learned how to speak. In fact, she learned how to speak English, French and German. She was an amazing person!

2. What is the main idea of this story?

_____

_____

_____

Skunks use a spray to protect themselves. This smelly spray can drive off animals and people. Skunks can squirt this liquid up to ten feet away. The odor is awful. But it helps to keep other dangerous animals away.

3. What is the main idea of this story?

_____

_____

_____

GO ON

Exploring Comprehension Skills 4, SV 9781419030925

Prewriting

≋ Think of a main idea that you would like to write about, such as an important person or an animal. Fill in the chart below.

Main Idea

Detail

Detail

Detail

On Your Own

≋ Now use another sheet of paper to write your story. Underline the sentence that tells the main idea.

Unit 5

What Is a Conclusion?

A conclusion is a decision you make after thinking about what you have read. In a story, the writer may not state all of his or her ideas. When you read, you often have to hunt for clues so that you can understand the whole story. By putting all of the writer's clues together, you can draw a conclusion about something that the writer has not stated.

There are many stories in this unit. You will draw conclusions based on each story that you read.

Try It!

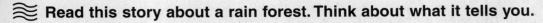 **Read this story about a rain forest. Think about what it tells you.**

> The climate around the equator is always warm. Much of the land is covered with rain forests. It rains in these areas every day. Some land gets more than five hundred inches of rain a year. September and March are the wettest and warmest times of the year.

What conclusion can you draw? Write your conclusion on the lines.

_____

_____

You might have written something such as "It is warm and wet in the rain forests" or "It is never cold in the rain forests." You can draw these conclusions from the paragraph. The first sentence tells about the warm climate around the equator. The second sentence says that it rains every day. From those clues, you can draw these conclusions.

GO ON

Exploring Comprehension Skills 4, SV 9781419030925

Practice Drawing Conclusions

This unit asks you to draw conclusions by using the clues in the stories. Look at the example below. Then darken the circle by the correct answer.

> In 1958 there was an earthquake in Springhill, Canada. There were 69 men trapped in the mine near town. The rescue workers dug fast and hard. But by the sixth day, few family members came to the mine. The sad rescue workers shook their heads but kept on digging. Then a voice was heard through an air pipe. "There are 12 of us in here. Please rescue us."

1. From this story, you can tell that
   Ⓐ Springhill was a big city.
   Ⓑ the people thought the men were dead.
   Ⓒ it was snowing during the earthquake.
   Ⓓ no one cared about the miners.

The correct answer is **B**. The story says, "But by the sixth day, few family members came to the mine. The sad rescue workers shook their heads but kept on digging." From these clues, you can conclude that the men were not expected to be found alive.

Sometimes a question will ask about something that you *cannot* tell from a story. Read the example that follows.

> Llamas are members of the camel family. But they look more like sheep. They have long necks and big ears. They live in the Andes Mountains. The owners get wool, meat, and milk from the llamas.

2. From this story, you <u>cannot</u> tell
   Ⓐ where llamas live.
   Ⓑ what owners get from the llamas.
   Ⓒ how many years llamas live.
   Ⓓ what llamas look like.

The story tells you what llamas look like, where they live, and what the owners get from the llamas. The story does not tell how many years llamas live. So the correct answer is **C**.

Name _____   Date _____

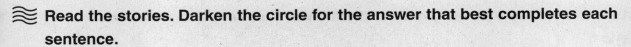 **Read the stories. Darken the circle for the answer that best completes each sentence.**

Baseball is a big sport in Japan. The rules are the same as those in America. But the customs are different. Players in Japan don't show their anger when they're out. They don't try to hurt the player from the other team as the player slides into second base. Also, when the fans clap, the players bow to them.

1. From this story, you can tell that
   Ⓐ Japanese players do not slide into second base.
   Ⓑ American players show their anger.
   Ⓒ Japanese players can play better.
   Ⓓ Japanese players wave when the fans clap.

Even though she had read the signs, Sally leaned over the bar. She stretched out her hand with the popcorn held lightly with her fingertips. The mouth of the striped animal just fit through the bars and reached the popcorn. It nibbled greedily.

2. From this story, you can tell that Sally
   Ⓐ is buying popcorn at the movies.
   Ⓑ can't read the signs she has seen.
   Ⓒ is feeding an animal at the zoo.
   Ⓓ once owned the striped animal.

Long ago Spanish ships sailed to America. They landed in a warm part of the country. The sun shone brightly there. Flowers bloomed even in the winter. There wasn't any snow. The Spanish people called the land *Florida*. It is the Spanish word for "blooming." That's how the state got its name.

3. From this story, you can tell that
   Ⓐ American states can have Spanish names.
   Ⓑ the Spanish people came in the spring.
   Ⓒ *Florida* means "snow" in Spanish.
   Ⓓ the Spanish ships landed in Texas.

Lesson 2

≈ **Read the stories. Darken the circle for the answer that best completes each sentence.**

Sid paid his fare and found a seat. He looked out the window as he passed street after street. When a woman with a baby got on, he got up and gave her his seat. He was glad that his ride was short.

1. You can tell that Sid is
   Ⓐ on a plane.
   Ⓑ in a taxi.
   Ⓒ on a bus.
   Ⓓ on a boat.

Fran marked her place and then closed the book. She put it on the table next to her bed. Then she fluffed up the pillow and set the alarm clock. She checked the window to make sure it was open. Then she crawled under the covers and fell asleep.

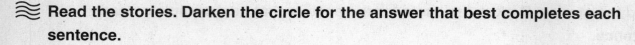

2. You can conclude that Fran
   Ⓐ finished reading her book.
   Ⓑ wanted some fresh air in the room.
   Ⓒ works in an office.
   Ⓓ leaves the porch light on at night.

Bonnie went to the post office to buy some stamps. But they didn't have the kind of stamps she wanted. So Bonnie bought another kind and mailed her letters. Then she went to the bank to get some wrappers for pennies. A worker told her that they were out of penny wrappers. So Bonnie decided to roll up her pennies on another day.

3. Bonnie's two errands were alike because
   Ⓐ she walked to both places.
   Ⓑ she bought something in both places.
   Ⓒ she used pennies in both places.
   Ⓓ neither place had what she wanted.

Name _____ Date _____

≋ **Read the stories. Darken the circle for the answer that best completes each sentence.**

Most desert plants have sharp stickers. These spines help the desert plant drink water. Morning mist forms big drops on these stickers. Then the drops fall, and the plant drinks the water. The spines also make the hot desert winds circle around the plant. This keeps the wind from taking the plant's water.

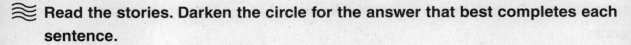

1. From this story, you can tell that
   Ⓐ most desert plants need spines to live.
   Ⓑ the spines on desert plants do not help them.
   Ⓒ desert plants do not live very long.
   Ⓓ the wind does not blow in the desert.

The War of 1812 was a strange war. It started when British ships stopped some American ships. The angry Americans warned the British to be careful. The British agreed to stop making so much trouble. But there were no telephones at that time. So the news didn't get to America very quickly. Just two days after the British agreed to stop causing trouble, the Americans started the war.

2. From this story, you can tell that
   Ⓐ telephones might have kept the war from starting.
   Ⓑ the Americans liked fighting wars back then.
   Ⓒ the Americans did not have very many ships.
   Ⓓ the Americans never warned the British.

"Don't jump!" the firefighters shouted. The woman stood at a window on the eleventh floor. The fire burned behind her. She was very scared.

The firefighters climbed to the twelfth floor. One of them found an old hose in the hallway. "Tie this to me," he said. "I'll climb out the window. She'll see that we're near, and maybe she won't jump." Because of this the woman's life was saved.

3. From this story, you can tell that
   Ⓐ the fire was on the twelfth floor of the building.
   Ⓑ the jump would have killed the woman.
   Ⓒ the woman had to go to the hospital.
   Ⓓ the woman wasn't scared at all.

95
Unit 5: Conclusion, Lesson 3
Exploring Comprehension Skills 4, SV 9781419030925

Name _____ Date _____

Lesson 4

≈ **Read the stories. Darken the circle for the answer that best completes each sentence.**

Wilbur Voliva believed that the earth was flat. He said that the sun was only three thousand miles away. He didn't believe that the sun was millions of miles away. In fact, Voliva didn't believe anything that scientists said. He also wanted to prove them wrong. So each year Voliva offered a big money prize. It was for anyone who could prove him wrong and show that the world was round.

1. From this story, you can tell that
   Ⓐ Voliva thought that the earth was round.
   Ⓑ scientists thought that the sun was millions of miles away.
   Ⓒ Voliva believed everything that scientists said.
   Ⓓ Voliva knew much about the sun.

Dan and Lola are married to each other. Both of them are truck drivers. They like driving trucks. They think that most truck drivers are fine people. But they also think that today truck drivers have a bad name. So Dan and Lola are working to get some laws passed. These laws would make truck drivers who drive too fast stay off the road.

2. From this story, you can tell that
   Ⓐ many truck drivers are married to each other.
   Ⓑ some truck drivers today drive too fast.
   Ⓒ most truck drivers carry food to other places.
   Ⓓ most truck drivers are bad people.

Grace could hardly wait until the fall. In fact, she was packed and ready to go. When the school year began, she would be in the United States. She would stay there for the full year. She felt lucky that she had been picked to study away from home. She would live with a family in Maine. Grace just knew she would like Maine.

3. From this story, you can tell that
   Ⓐ Grace is a good student.
   Ⓑ Grace does not live in the United States.
   Ⓒ Maine has many good schools.
   Ⓓ Grace will not miss her family.

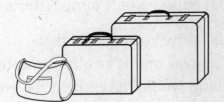

Name _____ Date _____

≋ **Read the stories. Darken the circle for the answer that best completes each sentence.**

The plant with the biggest seed in the world is called the coconut of the sea. Its huge seed can grow to be as big as a beach ball. It can weigh as much as fifty pounds.

1. From this story, you can tell that
   Ⓐ this plant probably grows in the United States.
   Ⓑ this seed wouldn't make a good beach ball.
   Ⓒ the seed is the size of a big orange.
   Ⓓ the seed tastes like coconut.

Let's say that you wanted to write down all the words while someone was talking. It would be very hard. People talk much faster than they write. But you could learn a special kind of writing. It's called shorthand. Shorthand doesn't look at all like the writing in this book. For instance, a straight line stands for *am*. So you'd have to learn to read shorthand, too.

2. From this story, you can tell that
   Ⓐ today many people are learning shorthand.
   Ⓑ shorthand is very easy to learn.
   Ⓒ the word *the* looks different in shorthand.
   Ⓓ people talk slower than they write.

Nellie Bly worked for a newspaper. She managed to report stories that nobody else could. Once she wanted to know how doctors treated the poor people. So she dressed in rags and pretended to be sick. She told them that she didn't have any money. She was taken to a hospital for the poor. There she had to sleep on the floor and eat terrible food. Later Nellie Bly wrote a story about her stay at this hospital. Her story surprised many people.

3. From this story, you can tell that
   Ⓐ some hospitals were not kind to the poor.
   Ⓑ Bly got sick when she was in the hospital.
   Ⓒ Bly won a prize for writing the story.
   Ⓓ the food at the hospital for the poor was good.

Lesson 6

≋ **Read the stories. Darken the circle for the answer that best completes each sentence.**

Did you know you can start a campfire with ice? First find a large piece of very clear ice. Then melt it down in the palms of your hands. When it is ready, the ice should look like a lens. It should have smooth curves on both sides. Finally use the ice to direct the sun's rays onto paper or wood shavings. This will start the fire.

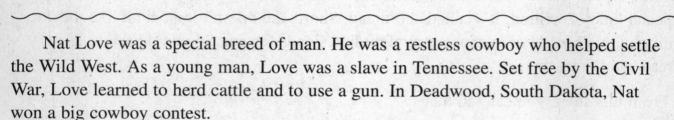

1. The story suggests that
   Ⓐ ice burns.
   Ⓑ the ice will freeze the fire.
   Ⓒ the warmth of your hands melts the ice.
   Ⓓ the ice should be curved on one side only.

Nat Love was a special breed of man. He was a restless cowboy who helped settle the Wild West. As a young man, Love was a slave in Tennessee. Set free by the Civil War, Love learned to herd cattle and to use a gun. In Deadwood, South Dakota, Nat won a big cowboy contest.

2. You can tell from the story that Nat Love
   Ⓐ drove a fast car.
   Ⓑ was a slave all his life.
   Ⓒ grew up in Texas.
   Ⓓ was a skilled cowboy.

Most whales survive by eating small sea creatures known as krill. Some companies were planning to harvest krill. Mary Cahoon and Mary McWhinnie were afraid that this harvest would cause whales to starve. They went to the South Pole to study the problem. They were the first women to spend a whole winter at the cold South Pole.

3. The story suggests that the companies
   Ⓐ planned to harvest wheat.
   Ⓑ weren't worried about whales.
   Ⓒ liked warm weather.
   Ⓓ went ice-skating often.

Name _____ Date _____

Lesson 7

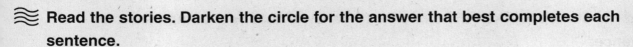 **Read the stories. Darken the circle for the answer that best completes each sentence.**

Today many men wear beards. But men have been shaving off their beards for thousands of years. At first the beard stood for manhood. Men shaved so that they could offer their beards to the gods. This was a sign of their obedience to the gods. The ancient soldiers were ordered not to wear beards. The beards could be grabbed very easily by enemy soldiers!

1. From the story, you <u>cannot</u> tell
   Ⓐ whether or not men still wear beards today.
   Ⓑ what the beard was a sign of at one time.
   Ⓒ why men shaved their beards long ago.
   Ⓓ whether or not soldiers today can wear beards.

When Tony woke up, he looked out the window. What luck! The mountain was covered with snow. Quickly he pulled on his long underwear and other warm clothes. He ate a good, hot breakfast so that he'd have plenty of energy. Then he checked his equipment. He clomped in his heavy boots toward the door and looked at the slopes.

2. In this story, the mood is
   Ⓐ angry.
   Ⓑ dangerous.
   Ⓒ happy.
   Ⓓ silly.

Nina was walking down a long hall. She kept turning corners and looking for a certain door. But all the doors she found were the wrong ones. Suddenly a bell rang, and Nina thought, "Oh, I must run, or I'll be late." But the bell kept ringing, and Nina couldn't run. Instead, she opened her eyes. The telephone beside her bed was ringing loudly.

3. From the story, you can tell that
   Ⓐ the telephone awoke Nina from her dream.
   Ⓑ Nina was in school.
   Ⓒ Nina didn't want to answer the telephone.
   Ⓓ Nina was glad the telephone rang.

Name _____ Date _____

Lesson 8

≈ **Read the stories. Darken the circle for the answer that best completes each sentence.**

Do you cover your mouth when you yawn? Today we think of this act as a part of good manners. But the early Romans covered their yawns out of fear. They thought that their souls might escape during a yawn. They believed that a hand to the lips kept them alive.

1. From the story, you can tell that
   - Ⓐ the Romans thought yawning caused death.
   - Ⓑ your teeth might fall out if you yawn.
   - Ⓒ yawns are bad for your health.
   - Ⓓ the Romans slept much of the time.

Valentina Tereshkova was nervous. She knew she'd soon make history. It was a still morning in 1963. She sat strapped in her seat. At last the Soviet spaceship began to shake. Its great engines roared. The ship climbed from the launch pad. It built up speed. Soon it was racing through the sky. Within minutes Valentina had become the first woman in space.

2. The story does <u>not</u> tell
   - Ⓐ when Tereshkova made her flight.
   - Ⓑ how Tereshkova gained fame.
   - Ⓒ how long it took Tereshkova to become famous.
   - Ⓓ how many people went with Tereshkova.

Stephen Hawking is a famous scientist. He has written books about physics and our universe. But Hawking must do all his work in a wheelchair. In his twenties, he found out he had Lou Gehrig's disease. Later, he lost his power to speak and write. Now he does his work on a special computer. The computer allows him to speak and type.

3. The story suggests that Stephen Hawking
   - Ⓐ is a baseball player.
   - Ⓑ uses a computer to walk.
   - Ⓒ can't use a regular computer.
   - Ⓓ likes to play video games.

100

Name _____   Date _____

≋ **Read the stories. Darken the circle for the answer that best completes each sentence.**

Karen could not walk or dance. But she loved to move in her wheelchair while she listened to music. Her favorite singer was Elvis Presley. One day she decided she would become his pen pal. She wrote a letter to Elvis and mailed it. Days went by, and no reply came. At first, Karen feared that Elvis might not write. But she kept hoping. At last the special letter came. It was the first of many.

1. The story suggests that Karen
   Ⓐ did not know how to write.
   Ⓑ lost her letter at the post office.
   Ⓒ became a pen pal with Elvis.
   Ⓓ lost all her hope.

Don't you wish you could break free of Earth's gravity? Then you could float in space. Spaceships have to break free of Earth's gravity to reach space. They must go very fast. In fact, they must travel at seven miles per second to break Earth's pull. That is about twenty-five thousand miles per hour.

2. The story does <u>not</u> tell
   Ⓐ how fast spaceships must go to reach space.
   Ⓑ what happens if a spaceship goes too slowly.
   Ⓒ that spaceships break free of Earth's pull.
   Ⓓ that you could float in space.

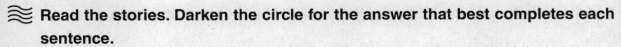

As a lawyer, Thurgood Marshall worked in many civil rights trials. He believed in "equal justice under the law." Marshall tried hard to gain that goal. He won many cases. He helped win equal rights for all Americans. Marshall's hard work paid off. First he was made a judge. Then he was picked to serve on the highest court in the land. He was made a Supreme Court justice. He became the first African American to hold that post.

3. You can tell from the story that Marshall
   Ⓐ was never a judge.
   Ⓑ did not work hard as a lawyer.
   Ⓒ mainly worked in traffic court.
   Ⓓ believed in equal rights for all.

101

Lesson 10

≋ **Read the stories. Darken the circle for the answer that best completes each sentence.**

A ship's speed was once figured by using a log. A log was thrown overboard at the front of the boat. Then time was kept until the log passed the stern, or rear. The length of the ship was known. So the captain would know how long the ship took to travel its length. The speed would be written in a *logbook*. That name is still used for the diary of a ship.

1. The story does <u>not</u> tell
   Ⓐ what kind of tree the log came from.
   Ⓑ how a ship's speed was once figured.
   Ⓒ what the captain would write the speed in.
   Ⓓ where the log was thrown overboard.

For years traveling farm workers were not treated well. At last César Chávez could stand no more. He thought farm workers should be paid more. He wanted better working conditions for them. To gain these, he formed a union. The group went on strike against grape growers in 1965. The strike lasted for five years. But finally their demands were met.

2. The story suggests that César Chávez
   Ⓐ thought farm workers were paid too much.
   Ⓑ grew tired of the bad treatment of farm workers.
   Ⓒ worked in rice fields.
   Ⓓ did not win the strike.

In 1814 much of Washington, D.C., was burned by the British. They burned the president's home, too. But Americans rebuilt the capital. The burned boards of the president's home were painted a bright white. Since then the mansion has been known as the White House.

3. You can tell from the story
   Ⓐ that the White House was once blue.
   Ⓑ how long the city took to rebuild.
   Ⓒ why the British burned the city.
   Ⓓ how the White House got its name.

Name _____   Date _____

≋ **Read the stories. Darken the circle for the answer that best completes each sentence.**

Francis Marion was a small, thin man. But he became a hero of the American Revolution. He set up his base in a South Carolina swamp. From there his soldiers launched raids on British camps. They caused the British troops all sorts of trouble. Marion's plans were always sly. Because of this he became known as the Swamp Fox.

1. From the story you can tell
   Ⓐ when the American Revolution was fought.
   Ⓑ that Francis Marion tricked British troops.
   Ⓒ that Francis Marion was captured.
   Ⓓ how many British camps Marion's men raided.

Tooth care has always been important. The oldest known tooth care product was a "chew stick." It was used in Egypt five thousand years ago. This stick was rubbed on the teeth to clean them. Today's toothbrush has bristles. This type of brush was first used in China around A.D. 1500. Hog bristles were used at first. Now nylon bristles are used.

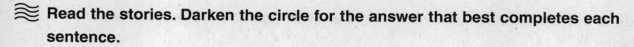

2. The story suggests that
   Ⓐ nylon bristles were first used around A.D. 1500.
   Ⓑ hog bristles are mostly used now.
   Ⓒ most people never use toothbrushes.
   Ⓓ the chew stick did not have bristles.

The Aztecs lived in ancient Mexico. They believed that their god had four sons. When one son would try to rule the earth, the others would fight him. So life on the earth was destroyed four times. At last, in the fifth age, the brothers agreed to rule together.

3. You can tell from the story that
   Ⓐ the four brothers fought often.
   Ⓑ the brothers were always friendly.
   Ⓒ none of the brothers wanted to rule the earth.
   Ⓓ the brothers finally agreed in the fourth age.

Lesson 12

≈ **Read the stories. Darken the circle for the answer that best completes each sentence.**

Scientists know that our universe is very old. Most think it is about 15 billion years old. Suppose that all that time added up to one year. This would mean that the dinosaurs lived in mid-December. Humans would have been on earth for a few minutes. Also, your life would be just two seconds long!

1. The story suggests that the human race is
   Ⓐ older than the universe.
   Ⓑ much younger than the universe.
   Ⓒ older than the dinosaurs.
   Ⓓ only two weeks old.

In Navajo legends, the first ones on Earth were First Man, First Woman, and Coyote. They lived in the first world and then in the second world. Later they moved to the third world. A water monster lived in the third world. Coyote stole two of the monster's children. The monster grew angry and caused the water to rise. First Man, First Woman, and Coyote then had to escape to the fourth world.

2. You <u>cannot</u> tell from the story
   Ⓐ who the first ones on Earth were.
   Ⓑ in which world the water monster lived.
   Ⓒ who caused the water to rise.
   Ⓓ why Coyote stole the water monster's children.

Stars do not last forever. After billions of years, they just burn out. Some stars suddenly brighten before they dim. These stars are called novas. *Nova* means "new" in Latin. The novas seem to be new stars. The last great nova was in 1054. It could be seen even in the daytime. It outshone everything in the sky except the sun and moon.

3. You can tell from the story that
   Ⓐ novas are not seen very often.
   Ⓑ great novas happen all the time.
   Ⓒ all stars become novas.
   Ⓓ the nova of 1054 was not very bright.

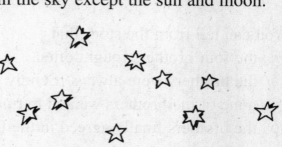

104

Name _____ Date _____

≈ **Read the stories. Darken the circle for the answer that best completes each sentence.**

About two hundred years ago, a doctor climbed a mountain in Europe. In those days, people never climbed mountains. They did not know what the tops of mountains were like. In fact they thought the doctor would meet many terrible monsters along the way. He came back down, safe and sound. He hadn't seen a single monster. Today many people enjoy the sport of mountain climbing.

1. From this story, you can tell that
   Ⓐ there are monsters living on mountains.
   Ⓑ there were trees on top of the mountain.
   Ⓒ others began climbing mountains after the doctor returned.
   Ⓓ the doctor was hurt during his climb.

Ants help keep one tree in South America safe. This tree has thorns that are hollow. The ants live inside the thorns. When animals try to eat the tree leaves, the ants rush out from the thorns. Hundreds of ants bite the animal. The thorns also stick the animal until it moves away.

2. From this story, you can tell that
   Ⓐ the tree and the ants need each other.
   Ⓑ ants eat other animals for food.
   Ⓒ the tree in this story is very tall.
   Ⓓ the thorns don't hurt the animals.

Baby Dee woke up and started crying loudly. Scott ran to her from the kitchen. He held Dee and talked to her. Scott didn't know why she was crying. He had fed Dee earlier. He checked to see if the baby's clothes were wet. But they were dry. Then Scott noticed an open safety pin lying in Dee's bed.

3. From this story, you can tell that
   Ⓐ the baby was probably very hungry.
   Ⓑ the safety pin probably hurt Dee.
   Ⓒ Scott had to take care of only one child.
   Ⓓ Scott was not a good father.

www.harcourtschoolsupply.com
© Harcourt Achieve Inc. All rights reserved.
105
Unit 5: Conclusion, Lesson 13
Exploring Comprehension Skills 4, SV 9781419030925

Lesson 14

≋ **Read the stories. Darken the circle for the answer that best completes each sentence.**

Joey baked some cornbread. He mixed cornmeal, flour, eggs, milk, baking powder, and butter. Then he put the cornbread in the oven for thirty minutes. When it was done, it was two inches high. Joey liked it so much that he made some more cornbread. But this time he forgot to mix in the baking powder. The cornbread came out flat. It looked like a tortilla!

1. From this story, you can tell that
   Ⓐ Joey had never baked cornbread before.
   Ⓑ the baking powder made the cornbread rise.
   Ⓒ cornbread was Joey's favorite thing to cook.
   Ⓓ Joey made tortillas often.

Dr. Cam treated sick cats in their homes. One day a woman asked him to look at her big orange cat. The cat hid under the bed when it heard the doctor coming. Dr. Cam and the woman crawled under the bed to catch the cat.

Dr. Cam shouted, "I've got the cat!"

But the woman yelled, "Ouch!"

2. From this story, you can tell that
   Ⓐ the orange cat hid under the bed often.
   Ⓑ the doctor didn't like orange cats.
   Ⓒ the doctor grabbed the woman's hair.
   Ⓓ the orange cat was glad to see the doctor.

Harold and June planted corn and carrots. June planted marigolds nearby. "I'm glad that marigold plants help keep bugs away from the other plants," she said.

"Just keep the vegetables away from the black walnut tree," Harold said. "Last year we planted seeds near it. Hardly anything came up there. But the rest of the garden did well."

3. From this story, you can tell that
   Ⓐ the bugs liked to eat the marigolds.
   Ⓑ some plants can help or hurt other plants.
   Ⓒ marigolds are red and orange bugs.
   Ⓓ many vegetables grew near the walnut tree.

Name _____   Date _____

Writing

≈ **Read the story. What conclusions can you draw? Use the clues in the story to answer the questions in complete sentences.**

The airplane ride took four hours. Laree's grandmother was waiting for her at the gate. Laree was glad to see her grandmother, but Midway Park was the real reason for the visit. She wanted to ride the Tytanic. It was supposed to be the biggest ride of its kind in the world. Laree knew she would get wet. She might even get soaked. Still she could not wait. Her school friends wanted to hear about the ride, and Laree planned to call them.

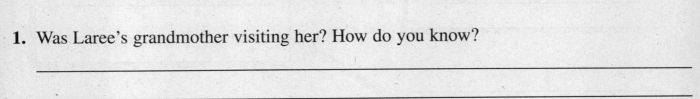

1. Was Laree's grandmother visiting her? How do you know?

_____

_____

2. Is Laree a student? How do you know?

_____

_____

3. Is the Tytanic a water ride? How do you know?

_____

_____

4. Do Laree's friends live near Laree's grandmother? How do you know?

_____

_____

Prewriting

≋ Think of a conclusion you can make about a person you know or something that you like to do. Write it in the conclusion box. Fill in the chart with some clues that could help another person make the same conclusion.

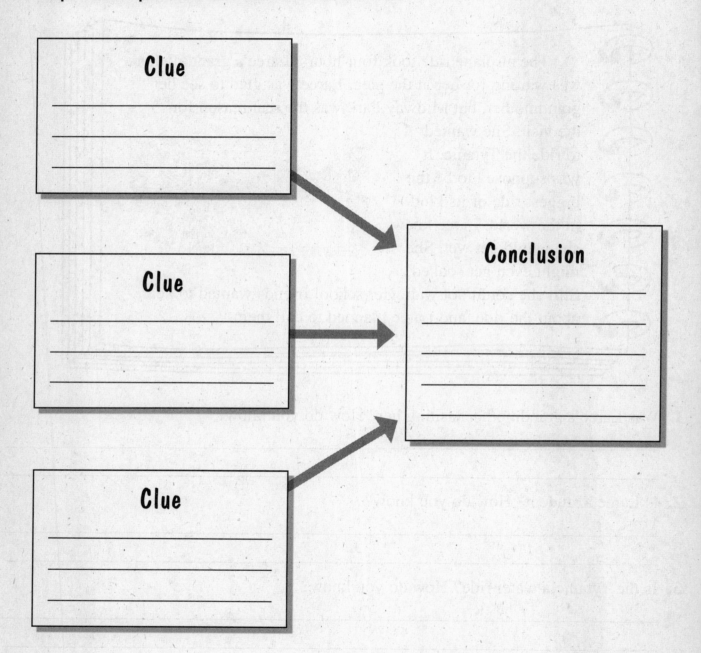

On Your Own

≋ Now use another sheet of paper to write a paragraph to describe the person or thing you like to do. Remember, don't state the conclusion. Just use the clues from above.

Name _____   Date _____

What Is an Inference?

An inference is a guess you make after thinking about what you already know. Suppose a friend invites you to a picnic. From what you know about picnics, you might infer that there will be food and drinks, and you will eat outside.

An author does not write every detail in a story. If every detail were told, a story would be long and boring. The main point would be lost. Suppose you read, "Lynn went to a restaurant." The writer does not have to tell you what a restaurant is. You already know that it is a place where people go to eat a meal. From what you know, you might imagine that Lynn looked at a menu. Then a server took her order. By filling in these missing details, you could infer that Lynn went to the restaurant to eat. You can infer this by putting together what you read and what you already know.

Try It!

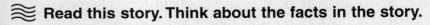 **Read this story. Think about the facts in the story.**

> Earthquakes can cause a lot of damage. This is especially true in places where the soil is loose and damp. An earthquake can turn loose, damp soil into thick mud. Buildings will sink or fall down. Many people may be hurt.

What can you infer? Write an inference on the lines below.

_____

_____

You might have written something such as "An earthquake can harm a city." You can make this inference from what the story tells you about earthquakes and what you already know.

109

Practice Making Inferences

In lessons 1 through 7 of this unit, you will be asked to answer the question "Which of these sentences is probably true?" Read the following story. Then darken the circle by the correct answer.

> Red-crowned cranes are beautiful birds. They are known for their trumpeting call. Many of these cranes live on an island in Japan. They live in marshes and are protected by law. But there are fewer than two thousand cranes left. They are in danger of disappearing.

1. Which of these sentences is probably true?
   Ⓐ The Japanese don't care about these cranes.
   Ⓑ People in Japan want to help the cranes.
   Ⓒ Red-crowned cranes live in the desert.
   Ⓓ There are too many cranes in Japan.

Only one answer is a good choice. Read answer **B**. It is the best choice. The story says that these cranes are in danger of disappearing and that they are protected by law. From the story, you can infer that people in Japan want to help these cranes.

In lessons 8 through 14 of this unit, you will do a new kind of exercise. Each story is followed by statements. Some of the statements are inferences. Others are facts. Decide whether each statement is an inference or a fact. Read this story. Then decide whether each statement is a fact or an inference. Darken the circle for your choice.

> Ben moved from England to Maine. In England he was taught to stand up when answering a question. So in his new class, he stood up when the teacher called on him. Some of the other students laughed at him. After class the teacher told him that he could stay in his seat when she called on him.

2. FACT   INFERENCE
   ○   ○   A. Ben was a polite person.
   ○   ○   B. Ben moved from England to Maine.
   ○   ○   C. The teacher wanted to help Ben.
   ○   ○   D. Some students laughed at Ben.

Statements **B** and **D** are in the story. They are facts. We can infer from the way he acts that Ben is a polite person. But this isn't stated in the story. So **A** is an inference. We can guess from the teacher's actions that she wanted to help Ben. So **C** is an inference.

Lesson 1

≈ **Read the stories. Darken the circle for the sentence that best answers each question.**

Ichabod Crane listened politely as the old man spoke. His voice was full of fear. He told Crane about a ghost. It was called the Headless Horseman. The ghost scared people who entered a place called Sleepy Hollow after dark. Crane laughed to himself as he listened to the story. That night Crane took a shortcut through Sleepy Hollow. Before he knew it, the ghost was chasing him.

1. Which of these sentences is probably true?
   Ⓐ The old man lived in Sleepy Hollow.
   Ⓑ Crane did not believe the man's story.
   Ⓒ Sleepy Hollow was far away.
   Ⓓ Crane liked to be scared.

The cowbird does not build a nest of its own. The mother cowbird lays her eggs in the nest of another bird. Then the cowbird leaves the eggs. She hopes the other bird will take care of her babies when they hatch.

2. Which of these sentences is probably true?
   Ⓐ The cowbird is lazy.
   Ⓑ Nests are hard to build.
   Ⓒ The cowbird is very caring.
   Ⓓ Baby cowbirds eat much food.

The game was almost over. The Mudville team was losing, but Casey was the next batter. He was the best hitter on the team. The Mudville crowd roared as the pitcher threw one strike, then another. If Casey missed one more pitch, he would strike out. The pitcher threw again, and the Mudville crowd grew very quiet. Casey walked away from the plate.

3. Which of these sentences is probably true?
   Ⓐ Casey hit the ball over the fence.
   Ⓑ The crowd forgot to cheer.
   Ⓒ Casey's team won the game.
   Ⓓ On the last pitch, Casey struck out.

Lesson 2

≋ **Read the stories. Darken the circle for the sentence that best answers each question.**

Jim Smiley thought he was smarter than anyone else. Jim liked to be in contests, and he almost always won them. One day a new man arrived in town. This stranger offered to have a frog-jumping contest with Jim. Jim agreed and said he would find a good frog for the stranger. While Jim was gone, the stranger tied small weights to the legs of Jim's frog. Soon Jim returned with the stranger's frog.

1. Which of these sentences is probably true?
   Ⓐ Jim's frog won the contest.
   Ⓑ The stranger's frog won the contest.
   Ⓒ Jim's frog jumped farther than it ever had.
   Ⓓ The frog tricked the stranger.

May Pierstorff took a strange trip in 1914. May's parents wanted her to visit her grandparents. They lived one hundred miles away. But a train ticket for May cost too much money. So her parents sent her by mail! It cost them 53 cents. May passed all the rules for being mailed. So May rode in the train mail car. She arrived safely.

2. Which of these sentences is probably true?
   Ⓐ May's parents wanted to save money.
   Ⓑ May didn't want to visit her grandparents.
   Ⓒ May was lost in the mail.
   Ⓓ May tried to walk to her grandparents' house.

One day Ann heard her friend Tom talking. Tom was telling everybody how smart his dog was. Tom said his dog could do tricks and could even ride a bicycle. But Ann knew that Tom's dog was just like any other dog. So Ann just smiled as Tom went on talking.

3. Which of these sentences is probably true?
   Ⓐ Ann didn't understand Tom's story.
   Ⓑ Tom wanted to make Ann mad at him.
   Ⓒ Ann didn't want to hurt Tom's feelings.
   Ⓓ Tom had two dogs and a cat.

Name _____   Date _____

≋ **Read the stories. Darken the circle for the sentence that best answers each question.**

The day was sunny and hot. Ava stood happily at the side of the swimming pool. She thought about the clear, blue water. Then she jumped in. But as she began swimming, she started shaking, and her skin began to turn blue.

1. Which of these sentences is probably true?
   Ⓐ The water was very hot.
   Ⓑ Ava forgot to wear her coat.
   Ⓒ The water was very cold.
   Ⓓ Ava didn't know how to swim.

When Louisa May Alcott was four, she had a birthday party. Many children were invited. Each child was supposed to get a small cake as a treat. Louisa handed out the cakes. She soon noticed that there were not enough cakes for everyone. One little girl was left in line, and there was only one cake left. Louisa wanted the cake for herself. But she smiled and gave the last cake to her friend.

2. Which of these sentences is probably true?
   Ⓐ The last little girl wanted two cakes.
   Ⓑ Louisa was kind and sharing.
   Ⓒ The last little girl was not hungry.
   Ⓓ Louisa was not very friendly.

Nick sat trembling behind the couch as a storm roared outside. Lightning flashed and thunder rumbled. Each time the thunder rolled, Nick screamed loudly. Nick's dad tried to get the boy to come out, but Nick would not move.

3. Which of these sentences is probably true?
   Ⓐ Storms made Nick's dad afraid.
   Ⓑ Nick liked to play hide-and-seek.
   Ⓒ Nick's dad made him feel better.
   Ⓓ Nick was afraid of thunder and lightning.

www.harcourtschoolsupply.com
113
Unit 6: Inference, Lesson 3
Exploring Comprehension Skills 4, SV 9781419030925

Lesson 4

≋ **Read the stories. Darken the circle for the sentence that best answers each question.**

At last the time came for Amy to give her report. She had to stand in front of the whole class and tell them about spiders. As she stood up, she dropped her report. The pages scattered all across the floor. Amy could feel everyone staring at her as she picked up the mess. Finally she reached the front of the room. She looked out at the class. Amy could feel her face turning red. She tried to speak, but no words would come out of her mouth.

1. Which of these sentences is probably true?
   Ⓐ Amy was in the wrong class.
   Ⓑ The class was afraid of Amy.
   Ⓒ Talking in front of people was hard for Amy.
   Ⓓ Amy knew nothing about spiders.

It was a cold day, and Ali stared at the white snow that covered the sidewalk. He knew he had a lot of shoveling to do. He was supposed to clean off the whole sidewalk. Out in the street, Ali's friends were pulling their sleds. Ali knew they were going to have fun sledding down the hill. They called for him to come, but Ali just waved. As they walked away, Ali slowly started to shovel.

2. Which of these sentences is probably true?
   Ⓐ Ali would rather work than play.
   Ⓑ The other children didn't like Ali.
   Ⓒ Ali loved to shovel snow.
   Ⓓ When Ali had a job to do, he did it.

If you are sick and you cough or sneeze on someone, that person could get sick, too. But it is not really a good idea to stop yourself from sneezing. If you do, you could pull a muscle in your face. You could also make your nose bleed.

3. Which of these sentences is probably true?
   Ⓐ Sneezing makes your nose bleed.
   Ⓑ Stopping a sneeze could be harmful.
   Ⓒ You can get over a cold by not sneezing.
   Ⓓ Sneezing is good exercise for your face.

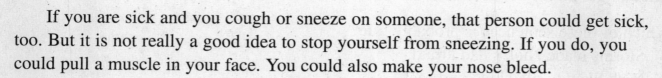

Lesson 5

≈ **Read the stories. Darken the circle for the sentence that best answers each question.**

Bob Hope was playing golf with a friend. His friend missed an easy shot. The angry friend threw his golf club into the tall grass. Bob secretly got the golf club back and started using it himself. Bob hit the ball a long way with his friend's club. The friend thought Bob's golf club was very good. He offered to buy it for fifty dollars. Bob sold the man the club he had just thrown away. Later Bob told his friend what had happened.

1. Which of these sentences is probably true?
   Ⓐ Bob decided to keep his friend's golf club.
   Ⓑ Bob's friend felt silly for buying back his own club.
   Ⓒ Bob used the money to open a golf shop.
   Ⓓ Bob's friend never played golf again.

Jo's mom was in the hospital. She had just had a new baby. Jo had seen the little thing with its wrinkled skin and its funny face. Jo was excited to have a new brother. But she was worried that her parents might not love her anymore.

2. Which of these sentences is probably true?
   Ⓐ Jo's parents needed to tell her they could love two children.
   Ⓑ Jo did not like wrinkles or funny faces.
   Ⓒ Jo's mother was at home.
   Ⓓ Jo wanted a dog instead of a new baby brother.

The president was coming to visit the small town. Everyone was very excited. All the people worked hard to clean up their town. They mowed the grass and swept the sidewalks. They fixed up the old houses. They even painted the water tower.

3. Which of these sentences is probably true?
   Ⓐ The president was moving to the town.
   Ⓑ The people were trying to fool the president.
   Ⓒ The president only liked big towns.
   Ⓓ The people wanted their town to look nice.

115

Name _____ Date _____

Lesson 6

≈ **Read the stories. Darken the circle for the sentence that best answers each question.**

Jim carefully lifted the eggs from their box. He handed two eggs to his mother. Then Jim measured a cup of milk, being careful not to spill any. He rubbed the cake pan with butter and watched as his mother poured in the batter. Then Jim and his mother cleaned up.

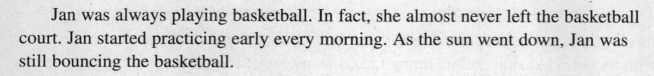

1. Which of these sentences is probably true?
   Ⓐ Jim was a good helper.
   Ⓑ Jim's mother was a bad cook.
   Ⓒ Jim was hungry.
   Ⓓ Jim's mother was lazy.

Jan was always playing basketball. In fact, she almost never left the basketball court. Jan started practicing early every morning. As the sun went down, Jan was still bouncing the basketball.

2. Which of these sentences is probably true?
   Ⓐ Jan slept at the basketball court.
   Ⓑ Tennis was very important to Jan.
   Ⓒ Jan wanted to be a great basketball player.
   Ⓓ The basketball was too big to bounce inside.

Nan was helping her uncle on the farm. He was loading the truck with hay for the cows. Nan's uncle threw a rope over the bales of hay. He told Nan to tie the rope carefully. But Nan only tied a loose knot. Then she hurried off to get a cool drink.

3. Which of these sentences is probably true?
   Ⓐ All the cool drinks were already gone.
   Ⓑ The rope tightened itself.
   Ⓒ The knot came untied.
   Ⓓ The cool drink made Nan sick.

Unit 6: Inference, Lesson 6
Exploring Comprehension Skills 4, SV 9781419030925

Name _____   Date _____

≋ **Read the stories. Darken the circle for the sentence that best answers each question.**

When his mother closed the door, Adam felt all alone. Adam was glad that the light by his bed was still on. Outside his window, dark shadows danced in the night sky. Adam decided to look under his bed. Then he got back in bed and pulled the covers over his head. At last he was able to close his eyes and fall asleep.

1. Which of these sentences is probably true?
   Ⓐ Adam felt safe when his mom was in the room.
   Ⓑ Going to sleep was easy for Adam.
   Ⓒ The shadows outside did not scare Adam.
   Ⓓ Adam thought his mother was under the bed.

The sport of softball began as indoor baseball. The first game of softball was played on a cold day in November 1887. It took place in a Chicago boat club. The men used an old boxing glove for a ball and a broomstick for a bat.

2. Which of these sentences is probably true?
   Ⓐ The men wanted to play baseball in the winter.
   Ⓑ Real baseballs cost a lot of money in 1887.
   Ⓒ The men didn't know how to play baseball.
   Ⓓ People first played softball inside.

Tom Sawyer stared at the long, wooden fence. His aunt had ordered him to paint it. But just the thought of all that work made Tom tired. Then he had a wonderful idea. As he began to paint, he acted as if he was having lots of fun. Other boys began to watch. They wanted to have fun, too. Soon Tom had all the other boys doing his work for him.

3. Which of these sentences is probably true?
   Ⓐ Working hard was fun for Tom.
   Ⓑ Tom didn't like fences.
   Ⓒ Tom's aunt painted the fence.
   Ⓓ Tom was a very tricky boy.

Name _____ Date _____

≈ **Read the stories. Darken the circle to show whether each statement is an inference or a fact.**

Have you ever caught fireflies on a warm summer night? Fireflies are interesting little insects. They make light with their bodies, but the light is not hot. Fireflies use their lights to send signals to other fireflies.

1. FACT INFERENCE

○   ○   **A.** Fireflies come out in summer.

○   ○   **B.** The light of fireflies is not hot.

○   ○   **C.** Fireflies send signals with their lights.

○   ○   **D.** Fireflies can only send signals at night.

A long time ago, no one knew that dinosaurs had ever lived. But in 1822 an English woman found a large tooth. In a few years, other parts of these large reptiles known as dinosaurs were found.

2. FACT INFERENCE

○   ○   **A.** Dinosaurs lived before 1822.

○   ○   **B.** Dinosaur bones were first found in England.

○   ○   **C.** A tooth was the first dinosaur bone found.

○   ○   **D.** Dinosaurs were reptiles.

William loved to go fishing. His grandfather had promised to take him on Saturday. That morning William packed a lunch and got his fishing pole ready. But about an hour before it was time to go, the phone rang. His grandfather said he was not feeling well and couldn't take William fishing. William was disappointed, but decided to make his grandfather a get-well card.

3. FACT INFERENCE

○   ○   **A.** William was a caring person.

○   ○   **B.** William loved to go fishing.

○   ○   **C.** William loved his grandfather.

○   ○   **D.** William's grandfather was sick.

Lesson 9

≋ **Read the stories. Darken the circle to show whether each statement is an inference or a fact.**

George Bidder was different from most boys his age. He was a whiz at math. When he was asked to work a math problem, he could do it in his head. Once he was told a 43-digit number backward. Right away he was able to switch it around in his head and say it forward in its correct order. He could even remember the number an hour later!

1. FACT INFERENCE

○ ○ **A.** George worked math problems in his head.
○ ○ **B.** Math was George's favorite subject.
○ ○ **C.** George was a math whiz.
○ ○ **D.** People thought George was very smart.

The city was full of people on their way home. Buses, trucks, cars, and taxis crowded the streets. Mark was in a hurry to catch the bus. As he ran up to the bus stop, the bus roared away. Mark sat down on a nearby bench and frowned.

2. FACT INFERENCE

○ ○ **A.** Mark ran to catch the bus.
○ ○ **B.** Mark was angry he missed the bus.
○ ○ **C.** The city streets were crowded.
○ ○ **D.** Mark was on his way home.

Sarah had not studied for the science test. Her friend Beth always did very well in science. Sarah sat beside Beth in class. When Mrs. Banes began passing out the science test, Sarah leaned over to Beth. "Write big so I can see," she whispered. Later, Mrs. Banes called the two girls to her desk.

3. FACT INFERENCE

○ ○ **A.** Sarah had not studied.
○ ○ **B.** The girls were caught cheating.
○ ○ **C.** Beth did well in science.
○ ○ **D.** Sarah whispered to Beth.

Lesson 10

≋ **Read the stories. Darken the circle to show whether each statement is an inference or a fact.**

It gets much hotter and much colder on the moon than here on Earth. At noon the temperature is four times higher on the moon than on Earth. For two weeks the moon stays dark all day long. This is called lunar night. At that time, it is four times colder than on Earth.

1. FACT INFERENCE

○ ○ **A.** The moon is coldest during lunar night.
○ ○ **B.** Lunar night lasts two weeks.
○ ○ **C.** The moon is hotter and colder than Earth.
○ ○ **D.** It is hottest on the moon at noon.

Miguel kicked the rocks in front of his feet. He had been excited about going to the rodeo. He wanted to see the cowboys do tricks. But now his mother wanted him to finish his farm work first. He slowly walked to the barn to water the horses. Then his brother's friend Ravon drove up in a truck. "How would you like a ride to the rodeo?" he asked.

2. FACT INFERENCE

○ ○ **A.** The horses were thirsty.
○ ○ **B.** Miguel was excited about going to the rodeo.
○ ○ **C.** Ravon drove up in a truck.
○ ○ **D.** Miguel did not finish his work.

Mount St. Helens is a volcano in Washington. In 1980 it erupted for the first time in over one hundred years. Fire and melting rock poured out of the volcano. This caused rivers to flood. Four states were covered with ash. More than sixty people were killed.

3. FACT INFERENCE

○ ○ **A.** Mount St. Helens erupted in 1980.
○ ○ **B.** The volcano did not erupt often.
○ ○ **C.** People lived near Mount St. Helens.
○ ○ **D.** Mount St. Helens is in Washington.

Name _____ Date _____

Lesson 11

≋ **Read the stories. Darken the circle to show whether each statement is an inference or a fact.**

Mushrooms grow under piles of fallen leaves or on dead logs. People eat mushrooms in spaghetti or on pizza, but not all mushrooms are good to eat. Some mushrooms have poison in them. The poisonous ones are called toadstools.

1. FACT   INFERENCE
○   ○   **A.** Some mushrooms are poisonous.
○   ○   **B.** People eat mushrooms on pizza.
○   ○   **C.** Mushrooms grow on dead logs.
○   ○   **D.** People should not eat toadstools.

Maggie, Lauren, and Sandra were playing basketball. Lauren ran down the court, bouncing the ball. As she tried to shoot a basket, Maggie pushed the ball away. It bounced off the court and hit a parked car nearby. The ball smashed the car's back window. Maggie began running away. "Let's get out of here!" she yelled to her friends.

2. FACT   INFERENCE
○   ○   **A.** Maggie was afraid.
○   ○   **B.** The ball smashed the window.
○   ○   **C.** Maggie didn't plan to hit the car.
○   ○   **D.** Lauren and Sandra didn't follow Maggie.

What happens if the arm of a starfish gets cut off? It grows a new one! The body of a starfish is shaped like a star. Each point is an arm. A starfish has eyes and feet on its arms. Its eyes are little spots on the end of its arms. The feet of a starfish are like tiny tubes under each arm.

3. FACT   INFERENCE
○   ○   **A.** A starfish has feet.
○   ○   **B.** Starfish can grow new arms.
○   ○   **C.** A starfish can see.
○   ○   **D.** Starfish are shaped like stars.

Name _____ Date _____

Lesson 12

≈ **Read the stories. Darken the circle to show whether each statement is an inference or a fact.**

Ted had been sick for a week. He had chicken pox. His teacher asked if anyone in the class could take Ted's homework to him. Dave had already had chicken pox, so he raised his hand. On his way to Ted's house, he bought some baseball cards for Ted.

1. FACT   INFERENCE
   ○   ○   **A.** Dave and Ted were friends.
   ○   ○   **B.** Ted had chicken pox.
   ○   ○   **C.** Dave raised his hand.
   ○   ○   **D.** Ted liked baseball cards.

People have used wheels for over five thousand years. They were probably first used in Middle Eastern countries. Chinese people learned to use the wheel about two thousand years later. Native Americans did not use wheels for work at that time. But they did put wheels on their toys.

2. FACT   INFERENCE
   ○   ○   **A.** Some Native American toys had wheels.
   ○   ○   **B.** People in China used wheels to do work.
   ○   ○   **C.** China is not in the Middle East.
   ○   ○   **D.** Wheels have been used for a long time.

"Come right home after school," Eva's mom told her.

"I will," said Eva. She waved goodbye and rode off on her bike to school. On her way home, Eva saw some of her friends at the park. They were riding their bikes through a mud puddle. It looked like fun. Eva decided to join them.

3. FACT   INFERENCE
   ○   ○   **A.** Eva rode her bike to school.
   ○   ○   **B.** Eva was late getting home.
   ○   ○   **C.** Eva's friends were at the park.
   ○   ○   **D.** Eva did not obey her mother.

Exploring Comprehension Skills 4, SV 9781419030925

Lesson 13

≋ **Read the stories. Darken the circle to show whether each statement is an inference or a fact.**

The Vikings were probably first to find North America. Ruins of Viking houses have been found in Newfoundland. Their houses were built around A.D. 1000. English fishers probably didn't reach that area until 1481. Columbus thought he was the first one to find the New World in 1492.

1. FACT   INFERENCE

○   ○   **A.** Vikings built houses about A.D. 1000.

○   ○   **B.** Newfoundland is in North America.

○   ○   **C.** Columbus didn't reach the New World first.

○   ○   **D.** Columbus didn't know about the Vikings.

Sitting Bull was born in South Dakota. He became a Sioux chief. It was a very hard time for his people. White settlers were moving onto his land. In 1868 the United States asked the Sioux and Cheyenne chiefs to sign a peace treaty. Many chiefs signed the treaty and lived on the reservation. But Sitting Bull did not. He wanted to live the old way.

2. FACT   INFERENCE

○   ○   **A.** Sitting Bull was a Sioux chief.

○   ○   **B.** Sitting Bull did not like the white settlers.

○   ○   **C.** Sitting Bull did not sign the treaty.

○   ○   **D.** Sitting Bull did not want to change.

When we think of windmills, we often think of Holland. The people there used windmills to take water off their land. That way they had more land for farming. Now windmills are used to make electricity.

3. FACT   INFERENCE

○   ○   **A.** There is not enough farmland in Holland.

○   ○   **B.** Farmland must be fairly dry.

○   ○   **C.** Holland has many windmills.

○   ○   **D.** Now windmills make electricity.

Lesson 14

≋ **Read the stories. Darken the circle to show whether each statement is an inference or a fact.**

"Don't you ever come here again!" Rosa shouted to her best friend Gail.

"I won't!" Gail shouted back. Gail slammed the front door shut as she left.

Soon Rosa was sorry for what she had said. She ran out the front door and headed toward Gail's house. Gail was running down the sidewalk to Rosa's house.

1. FACT   INFERENCE

○   ○   **A.** Rosa and Gail were best friends.

○   ○   **B.** Gail was coming to say she was sorry.

○   ○   **C.** Rosa shouted at Gail.

○   ○   **D.** Gail slammed the front door.

Have you ever wondered what it would be like to live in another country? Each year thousands of students from the United States do just that. They live in another country for a few months. Some even stay for a year. They live with a host family in the new country. The host family members try to make the student a part of their family life. The students go to school, make friends, visit new places, and eat new foods. Sometimes they even learn to speak another language.

2. FACT   INFERENCE

○   ○   **A.** Most host families speak English.

○   ○   **B.** Some students learn a new language.

○   ○   **C.** Host families like students from the United States.

○   ○   **D.** The students visit new places.

Rob heard a rooster crow. He opened his eyes and felt the sun shining through the window. It was his first day on his cousin's farm. He jumped out of bed and put on his jeans. When his aunt called him to breakfast, he ran downstairs eagerly.

3. FACT   INFERENCE

○   ○   **A.** Rob liked farm life.

○   ○   **B.** The sun was shining.

○   ○   **C.** Rob was hungry.

○   ○   **D.** A rooster crowed.

Name _____ Date _____

Writing

≋ **Read the story. What inferences can you make? Use the clues in the story to answer the questions in complete sentences.**

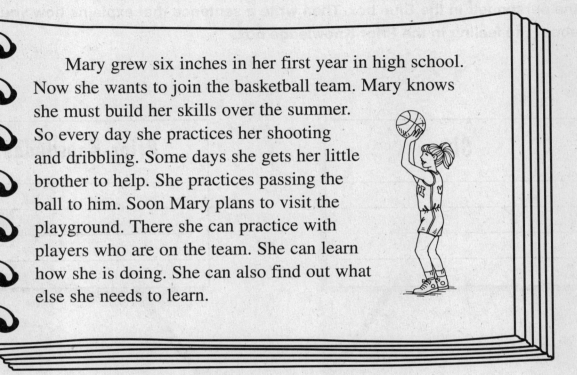

Mary grew six inches in her first year in high school. Now she wants to join the basketball team. Mary knows she must build her skills over the summer. So every day she practices her shooting and dribbling. Some days she gets her little brother to help. She practices passing the ball to him. Soon Mary plans to visit the playground. There she can practice with players who are on the team. She can learn how she is doing. She can also find out what else she needs to learn.

1. Why didn't Mary join the team in her first year?

_____

_____

2. What skill does Mary's little brother need to help Mary?

_____

_____

3. What kind of person is Mary?

_____

_____

4. How does Mary feel about her skills?

_____

_____

GO ON

Prewriting

≋ Think of a time when you saw someone who was very excited, scared, or angry. What did the person do that let you know how he or she was feeling? Write a sentence that states the person's feeling in the Inference box. Write the actions that told you how the person felt in the Clue box. Then write a sentence that explains how you know about the feeling in the Prior Knowledge box.

Clue

_____

_____

_____

_____

Prior Knowledge

_____

_____

_____

Inference

_____

_____

_____

_____

On Your Own

≋ Now use another sheet of paper to write a paragraph that tells about the feelings of the person from above. Remember, don't tell what the emotion was. Just use the clue and the prior knowledge to describe what you saw.

Exploring Comprehension Skills 4, SV 9781419030925

ANSWER KEY

Unit 1: Facts, Assessment, p. 5
1. D
2. D
3. A
4. C
5. B

Unit 2: Sequence, Assessment, p. 6
1. 1, 3, 2
2. A

Unit 3: Context, Assessment, p. 7
1. A
2. B
3. C
4. B
5. B
6. A

Unit 4: Main Idea, Assessment, p. 8
1. C
2. B
3. C

Unit 5: Conclusion, Assessment, p. 9
1. C
2. B
3. C

Unit 6: Inference, Assessment, p. 10
1. C
2. B
3. A. F   C. I
   B. F   D. F

Unit 1: Facts
Lesson 1, pp. 13–14
1. B   6. B
2. B   7. C
3. A   8. D
4. C   9. A
5. D   10. D

Lesson 2, pp. 15–16
1. A   6. A
2. A   7. D
3. C   8. C
4. D   9. B
5. D   10. D

Lesson 3, pp. 17–18
1. B   6. B
2. A   7. C
3. C   8. A
4. B   9. D
5. C   10. D

Lesson 4, pp. 19–20
1. C   6. A
2. D   7. D
3. C   8. D
4. B   9. C
5. D   10. B

Lesson 5, pp. 21–22
1. D   6. B
2. B   7. A
3. A   8. D
4. D   9. C
5. C   10. B

Lesson 6, pp. 23–24
1. B   6. C
2. B   7. D
3. A   8. C
4. D   9. D
5. B   10. B

Lesson 7, pp. 25–26
1. C   6. B
2. C   7. A
3. A   8. A
4. B   9. D
5. C   10. D

Lesson 8, pp. 27–28
1. C   6. C
2. D   7. D
3. B   8. D
4. A   9. B
5. D   10. A

Writing, pp. 29–30
Possible answers:
1. Mount Everest is five and one-half miles above sea level.
2. Mount Everest is north of India between Nepal and Tibet.
3. Sir Edmund Hillary and Tenzing Norgay were first to reach the top of Mount Everest.
Prewriting: Check students' answers.

Unit 2: Sequence
Lesson 1, p. 34
1. 2, 1, 3   4. B
2. C   5. C
3. A

Lesson 2, p. 36
1. 3, 2, 1   4. C
2. A   5. A
3. A

Lesson 3, p. 38
1. 2, 3, 1   4. B
2. A   5. C
3. C

Lesson 4, p. 40
1. 2, 1, 3   4. B
2. C   5. A
3. A

Lesson 5, p. 42
1. 3, 2, 1   4. B
2. C   5. A
3. A

Lesson 6, p. 44
1. 3, 1, 2   4. B
2. C   5. A
3. A

Lesson 7, p. 46
1. 1, 3, 2   4. B
2. C   5. A
3. A

Lesson 8, p. 48
1. 2, 3, 1   4. C
2. A   5. B
3. C

Writing, pp. 49–50
Possible answers:
1. She mixed dirt and sand after she filled the bottom of the bowl with rocks.
2. She added water after she covered the rocks with dirt and sand.
3. She put the bowl near a window after she planted ferns and moss.
4. The plants began to grow a few days later.
Prewriting: Check students' sequence and use of time order words.

Unit 3: Context
Lesson 1, p. 53
1. C   5. C
2. D   6. B
3. B   7. A
4. C   8. C

Lesson 2, p. 54
1. B   5. D
2. D   6. B
3. A   7. D
4. C   8. A

Lesson 3, p. 55
1. D   5. C
2. A   6. A
3. A   7. B
4. C   8. D

Lesson 4, p. 56
1. C   5. A
2. B   6. C
3. C   7. A
4. A   8. B

Lesson 5, p. 57
1. C   5. A
2. B   6. B
3. A   7. C
4. B   8. D

Lesson 6, p. 58
1. B   5. A
2. A   6. C
3. B   7. A
4. D   8. D

Lesson 7, p. 59
1. B   5. B
2. A   6. D
3. C   7. D
4. C   8. B

Lesson 8, p. 60
1. D   5. B
2. B   6. A
3. A   7. C
4. D   8. B

Lesson 9, p. 61
1. C   3. B
2. A   4. D

Lesson 10, p. 62
1. C   3. B
2. D   4. C

Lesson 11, p. 63
1. C   3. D
2. B   4. A

Lesson 12, p. 64
1. C   3. C
2. D   4. B

Lesson 13, p. 65
1. D   3. A
2. B   4. C

Lesson 14, p. 66
1. B   3. C
2. D   4. C

Lesson 15, p. 67
1. D   3. A
2. D   4. C

Lesson 16, p. 68
1. A   3. A
2. A   4. C

Exploring Comprehension Skills 4, SV 9781419030925

Writing, pp. 69–70
Possible answers:
1. wet or clean
2. dirt or mud
3. stars or moon
4. day or summer
5. class or school
6. sit or play

Prewriting: Check students' graphic organizers and paragraphs for the use of context clues.

Unit 4: Main Idea

Lesson 1, p. 73
1. A   2. C   3. B

Lesson 2, p. 74
1. B   2. C   3. B

Lesson 3, p. 75
1. C   2. B   3. B

Lesson 4, p. 76
1. C   2. C   3. A

Lesson 5, p. 77
1. B   2. C   3. A

Lesson 6, p. 78
1. A   2. A   3. B

Lesson 7, p. 79
1. A   2. A   3. A

Lesson 8, p. 80
1. A   2. B   3. A

Lesson 9, p. 81
1. B   2. C   3. D

Lesson 10, p. 82
1. C   2. A   3. D

Lesson 11, p. 83
1. A   2. C   3. B

Lesson 12, p. 84
1. C   2. A   3. B

Lesson 13, p. 85
1. C   2. B   3. A

Lesson 14, p. 86
1. C   2. D   3. B

Lesson 15, p. 87
1. B   2. A   3. B

Lesson 16, p. 88
1. C   2. C   3. A

Writing, pp. 88–90
Possible answers:
1. There is still a lot to learn about oceans.
2. Helen Keller was an amazing person.
3. Skunks protect themselves with a smelly spray.

Prewriting: Check students' main idea and details.

Unit 5: Conclusion

Lesson 1, p. 93
1. B   2. C   3. A

Lesson 2, p. 94
1. C   2. B   3. D

Lesson 3, p. 95
1. A   2. A   3. B

Lesson 4, p. 96
1. B   2. B   3. B

Lesson 5, p. 97
1. B   2. C   3. A

Lesson 6, p. 98
1. C   2. D   3. B

Lesson 7, p. 99
1. D   2. C   3. A

Lesson 8, p. 100
1. A   2. D   3. C

Lesson 9, p. 101
1. C   2. B   3. D

Lesson 10, p. 102
1. A   2. B   3. D

Lesson 11, p. 103
1. B   2. D   3. A

Lesson 12, p. 104
1. B   2. D   3. A

Lesson 13, p. 105
1. C   2. A   3. B

Lesson 14, p. 106
1. B   2. C   3. B

Writing, pp. 107–108
Possible answers:
1. No, Laree was visiting her grandmother. She got off the plane.
2. She is a student. She is planning to call her school friends.
3. The Tytanic is a water ride. Laree thinks she might get soaked.
4. Laree's friends don't live near her grandmother. They live at least four hours away.

Prewriting: Check students' clues and conclusion.

Unit 6: Inference

Lesson 1, p. 111
1. B   2. A   3. D

Lesson 2, p. 112
1. B   2. A   3. C

Lesson 3, p. 113
1. C   2. B   3. D

Lesson 4, p. 114
1. C   2. D   3. B

Lesson 5, p. 115
1. B   2. A   3. D

Lesson 6, p. 116
1. A   2. C   3. C

Lesson 7, p. 117
1. A   2. D   3. D

Lesson 8, p. 118
1. A. I   2. A. I   3. A. I
   B. F   B. I   B. F
   C. F   C. F   C. I
   D. I   D. F   D. F

Lesson 9, p. 119
1. A. F   2. A. F   3. A. F
   B. I   B. I   B. I
   C. F   C. F   C. F
   D. I   D. I   D. F

Lesson 10, p. 120
1. A. I   2. A. I   3. A. F
   B. F   B. F   B. I
   C. F   C. F   C. I
   D. I   D. I   D. F

Lesson 11, p. 121
1. A. F   2. A. I   3. A. F
   B. F   B. F   B. F
   C. F   C. I   C. I
   D. I   D. I   D. F

Lesson 12, p. 122
1. A. I   2. A. F   3. A. F
   B. F   B. I   B. I
   C. F   C. I   C. F
   D. I   D. F   D. I

Lesson 13, p. 123
1. A. F   2. A. F   3. A. I
   B. I   B. I   B. I
   C. I   C. F   C. I
   D. I   D. I   D. F

Lesson 14, p. 124
1. A. F   2. A. I   3. A. I
   B. I   B. F   B. F
   C. F   C. I   C. I
   D. F   D. F   D. F

Writing, pp. 125–126
Possible answers:
1. She thought she wasn't tall enough. She didn't think she played well enough.
2. He needs to be able to catch passes.
3. Mary is willing to learn, hard-working, and serious.
4. Mary is not certain about her skills. She seems to think she has more to learn.

Prewriting: Check students' clue, prior knowledge, and inference.

Exploring Comprehension Skills 4, SV 9781419030925